Introduction

Your child and her favorite 18" doll can play look-alike with the colorful knit sweater designs in this book.

We have provided instructions for each of the designs in both child size and doll size.

You'll find an extra warm and cozy hooded cardigan, six wearable pullovers and a brightly colored vest.

Your child or grandchild will be delighted to receive these matched sets as presents, and will be all smiles while modeling the sweaters with her miniature "best friend" dressed to look like a twin!

Contents

Preppy Placket Pullover

Sizes:

| 18" doll | 2 | 4 | 6 | 8 | 10 | 12 |

Finished Chest Size:

| 14" | 27" | 28½" | 30" | 32" | 34" | 36" |

Note: *Instructions are written for doll; changes for other sizes are in parentheses.*

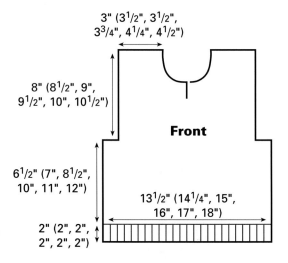

3" (3¹/₂", 3¹/₂", 3³/₄", 4¹/₄", 4¹/₂")

8" (8¹/₂", 9", 9¹/₂", 10", 10¹/₂")

Front

6¹/₂" (7", 8¹/₂", 10", 11", 12")

13¹/₂" (14¹/₄", 15", 16", 17", 18")

2" (2", 2", 2", 2", 2")

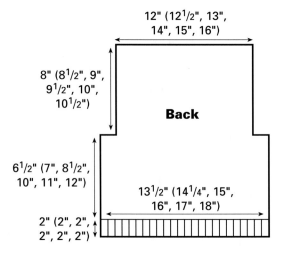

12" (12¹/₂", 13", 14", 15", 16")

8" (8¹/₂", 9", 9¹/₂", 10", 10¹/₂")

Back

6¹/₂" (7", 8¹/₂", 10", 11", 12")

13¹/₂" (14¹/₄", 15", 16", 17", 18")

2" (2", 2", 2", 2", 2")

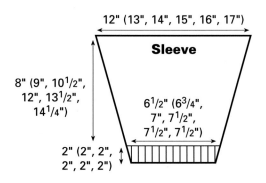

12" (13", 14", 15", 16", 17")

Sleeve

8" (9", 10¹/₂", 12", 13¹/₂", 14¹/₄")

6¹/₂" (6³/₄", 7", 7¹/₂", 7¹/₂", 7¹/₂")

2" (2", 2", 2", 2", 2")

These measurements for child's sweater sizes are approximate.

Materials:

Fine (sport weight) yarn, 2½ (7½, 7½, 10, 12½, 12½, 15) oz [168 (504, 504, 672, 840, 840, 1008) yds, 70 (210, 210, 280, 350, 350, 420) gms] off-white; 2½ oz, 168 yds, 70 gms lt brown (for all sizes)

Note: Our photographed sweaters were made with Lion Brand Micro Spun, French Vanilla #98 and Mocha #124.

Size 8 (5mm) straight knitting needles, or size required for gauge
Size 5 (3.75mm) straight knitting needle
Size 18 tapestry needle
Two buttons, ⅝"-diameter

Gauge:

With larger size needles in stockinette stitch (knit one row, purl one row):
5 sts = 1"

Special Abbreviations

Make 1 (M1):

Insert left needle from front to back under horizontal strand between the last stitch worked and the next stitch on the left needle; knit this strand through the back loop—M1 made.

Slip, Slip, Knit (SSK):

Slip next 2 sts one at a time from the left needle to the right needle, insert the left needle into the fronts of these two stitches and knit them together—SSK made.

Instructions

Back

With smaller size needles and lt brown, cast on 32 (62, 66, 68, 72, 78, 82) sts.

Ribbing:

Row 1 (right side): * K1, P1; rep from * across.

Rows 2 through 5 (15, 15, 15, 15, 15, 15): Rep Row 1.

Next Row: Continuing in pattern as established, work 4 (7, 6, 6, 4, 7, 5) sts, M1 (see Special Abbreviations); * work 6 (9, 9, 7, 8, 8, 19) sts, M1; rep from * 3, (5, 5, 7, 7, 7, 7) times more; work 4 (7, 6, 6, 4, 7, 5) sts—37 (69, 73, 77, 81, 87, 91) sts.

Change to larger size needles and off-white.

Body:

Row 1 (right side): Knit.

Row 2: Purl.

Rep Rows 1 and 2 until piece measures about 3" (8½", 9", 10½", 12", 13", 14") from cast-on edge, ending by working a wrong side row.

Armhole Shaping:

Row 1 (right side): Bind off 2 (4, 5, 5, 5, 5, 5) sts; knit across.

Row 2: Bind off 2 (4, 5, 5, 5, 5, 5) sts; purl across—33 (61, 63, 67, 71, 77, 81) sts.

Row 3: Knit.

Row 4: Purl.

Rep Rows 3 and 4 until piece measures about 6" (14½", 15½", 17½", 19½", 21", 22½") from cast-on edge, ending by working a wrong side row.

Bind off.

Front

With smaller size needles and lt brown, cast on 32 (62, 66, 68, 72, 78, 82) sts.

Ribbing:
Rows 1 through 5 (15, 15, 15, 15, 15, 15): Work same as rows 1 through 5 (15, 15, 15, 15, 15, 15) of Back.

Next Row: Continuing in pattern as established, work 4, (6, 6, 6, 4, 8, 6) sts, M1 (see Special Abbreviations); * work 8 (10, 11, 8, 9, 9, 10) sts, M1; rep from * 2 (4, 4, 6, 6, 6, 6) times more; work 4 (6, 5, 6, 5, 7, 6) sts—36 (68, 72, 76, 80, 86, 90) sts.

Change to larger size needles and off-white.

Body:
Row 1 (right side): Knit.

Row 2: Purl.

Rep Rows 1 and 2 until piece measures about 3" (8½", 9", 10½", 12", 13", 14") from cast-on edge, ending by working a wrong side row.

Armhole Shaping:
Row 1 (right side): Bind off 2 (4, 5, 5, 5, 5, 5) sts; knit across.

Row 2: Bind off 2 (4, 5, 5, 5, 5, 5) sts; purl across—32 (60, 62, 66, 70, 76, 80) sts.

Row 3: Knit.

Row 4: Purl.

Rep Rows 3 and 4 until piece measures about 4" (10½", 11¼", 13¾", 14½", 15¾", 16½") from cast-on edge, ending by working a wrong side row.

Placket Opening:
Row 1: For left shoulder, K14 (25, 26, 28, 30, 33, 35) sts; join second skein of off-white, for neck, bind off next 4 (10, 10, 10, 10, 10, 10) sts; for right shoulder, knit across—14 (25, 26, 28, 30, 33, 35) sts on each shoulder.

Note: Work both shoulders at same time with separate skeins of yarn.

Row 2: Purl across both shoulders.

Row 3: Knit across both shoulders.

Rep Rows 2 and 3 until piece measures about 5½" (13½", 14", 16", 18", 19½", 21½") from cast-on edge.

Neck Shaping:
Row 1 (right side): For left shoulder, K14 (25, 26, 28, 30, 33, 35) sts; for right shoulder bind off 6 (7, 6, 8, 8, 7, 7) sts; knit across.

Row 2: For right shoulder, P8 (18, 20, 20, 22, 26, 28) sts; for left shoulder, bind off 6 (7, 6, 8, 8, 7, 7) sts; purl across—8 (18, 20, 20, 22, 26, 28) sts on each shoulder.

For Doll Size Only:
See For All Sizes below.

For Sizes 2, 4, 6, 8, 10 and 12 Only:
Row 3: For left shoulder, knit to last 4 sts; K2 tog; K2; for right shoulder, K2, sl 1 as to purl, K1, PSSO; knit across—17 (19, 19, 21, 25, 27) sts on each shoulder.

Row 4: Purl across both shoulders.

Rows 5 through 6 (8, 8, 8, 10, 10): Rep Rows 3 and 4 once (twice, twice, twice, 3, 3) times more—16 (17, 17, 19, 22, 24) sts.

For All Sizes:
Next Row: Knit.

Next Row: Purl.

Rep last two rows until piece measures about 6" (14½", 15½", 17½", 19½", 21", 22½") from cast-on edge, ending by working a wrong side row.

Bind off.

Sew shoulder seams.

Sleeve

With smaller size needle and off-white, pick up 30 (60, 66, 70, 76, 80, 86) sts along armhole edge beginning and ending above bound off sts of armhole shaping and having same number of sts on front and back.

Change to larger size needles.

Row 1 (wrong side): Purl.

Row 2 (right side): Knit.

Rows 3 and 4: Rep Rows 1 and 2.

Row 5: Purl.

For Doll Size Only:
Row 6: K2, SSK (see Special Abbreviations), knit to last 4 sts; K2 tog; K2—28 sts.

Row 7: Purl.

Row 8: Knit.

Rows 9 and 10: Rep Rows 7 and 8.

Row 11: Purl.

Rows 12 through 30: Rep Rows 6 through 12 three times more. At end of Row 30—22 sts.

Row 31: Knit.

Row 32: Purl.

Rep Rows 31 and 32 until sleeve measures about 7", ending by working a wrong side row.

Continue with For All Sizes.

For Sizes 2, 4, 6, 8, 10 and 12 Only:

Row 6: K2, SSK (see Special Abbreviations), knit to last 4 sts; K2 tog; K2—58 (64, 68, 74, 78, 88) sts.

Row 7: Purl.

Row 8: Knit.

Row 9: Purl.

Rows 10 through 53 (61, 65, 73, 81, 93): Rep Rows 6 through 9 eleven (13, 14, 16, 18, 21) times more. At end of last row—36 (38, 40, 42, 42, 42) sts.

Rep Rows 8 and 9 until sleeve measures about 8" (9", 10½" 12", 13½", 14¼"), ending by working a wrong side row.

Next Row: K4 (5, 4, 5, 5, 5), K2 tog; * K7 (7, 8, 8, 8, 8) K2 tog; rep from * 3 times more; K3 (4, 4, 5, 5, 5)—32 (34, 36, 38, 38, 38) sts.

Continue with For All Sizes.

For All Sizes:

Change to smaller size needles and lt brown.

Ribbing:

Row 1 (right side): K1, P1; rep from * across.

Rep Row 1 until ribbing measures about 2", ending by working a wrong side row.

Bind off.

Rep for other sleeve.

Edgings

Neck Edging:
Hold piece with right side facing you and neck edge at top; with smaller size needles and lt brown pick up 6 (7, 6, 8, 8, 7, 8) sts across bound off sts; pick up 5 (9, 10, 10, 10, 12, 10) sts along right front neck edge; pick up 17 (29, 29, 31, 31, 31, 33) sts across back neck edge; pick up 5 (9, 10, 10, 10, 12, 10) sts along left front neck edge; pick up 6 (7, 6, 8, 8, 7, 8) sts across bound off sts—39 (61, 61, 67, 67, 69, 69) sts.

Row 1: K1; * P1, K1; rep from * across.

Row 2: P1; * K1, P1; rep from * across.

Rows 3 through 4 (6, 6, 6, 6, 6, 6): Rep Rows 1 and 2 once (twice, twice, twice, twice, twice, twice) more.

Bind off loosely in ribbing.

Left Front Placket Edging (button band):
Hold piece with right side of left front facing you; with smaller size needles and lt brown pick up 13 (17, 19, 23, 25, 27, 31) sts evenly spaced along center front placket edge.

Row 1: * K1, P1; rep from * across.

Row 2: * P1, K1; rep from * across.

Rows 3 through 4 (8, 8, 8, 8, 8, 8): Rep Rows 1 and 2 once (3, 3, 3, 3, 3, 3) times more.

Bind off loosely in ribbing.

Right Front Placket Edging (buttonhole band):
Hold piece with right side of right front facing you; with smaller size needles and lt brown pick up 13 (17, 19, 23, 25, 27, 31) sts along center front placket edge.

For Doll Size Only:

Row 1: P1; * K1, P1; rep from * across.

Row 2: Continuing in pattern, K1, P1; bind off 2 sts, work 5 sts, bind off 2 sts; work remaining sts.

Row 3: * Work in pattern to bound off sts; cast on 2 sts; rep from * once more; work remaining sts.

Row 4: K1; * P1, K1; rep from * across.

Bind off loosely in pattern.

Continue with Finishing below.

For Sizes 2, 4, 6, 8, 10 and 12 Only:

Row 1: P1; * K1, P1; rep from * across.

Row 2: K1; * P1, K1; rep from * across.

Row 3: Rep Row 1.

Row 4: Continuing in rib pattern, work 5 (5, 7, 7, 7, 7) sts, bind off 2 sts; * K5 (7, 9, 11, 13, 17) sts, bind off 2 sts; K5.

Row 5: * Work in pattern to bound off sts, cast on 2 sts; rep from * once more; work remaining sts.

Row 6: Rep Row 2.

Rows 7 and 8: Rep Rows 1 and 2.

Bind off loosely in ribbing.

Continue with Finishing.

Finishing

Step 1: Sew side edges at top of sleeve to bound off sts of front and back armholes.

Step 2: Sew sleeve and side seams.

Step 3: Place buttonhole band over button band and sew bottom edge through both thicknesses to sweater opening.

Step 4: Sew buttons to left front band under buttonholes.

Sunny Day Vest

■■■□ INTERMEDIATE

Sizes:

18" doll	2	4	6	8	10	12

Finished Chest Size:

14"	27"	28½"	30"	32"	34"	36"

Note: *Instructions are written for doll; changes for other sizes are in parentheses.*

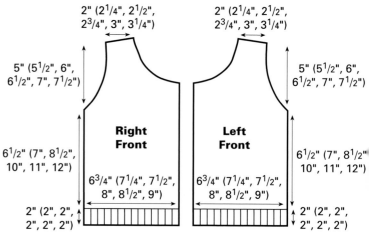

2" (2¼", 2½", 2¾", 3", 3¼")

2" (2¼", 2½", 2¾", 3", 3¼")

5" (5½", 6", 6½", 7", 7½")

5" (5½", 6", 6½", 7", 7½")

Right Front

Left Front

6½" (7", 8½", 10", 11", 12")

6½" (7", 8½", 10", 11", 12")

6¾" (7¼", 7½", 8", 8½", 9")

6¾" (7¼", 7½", 8", 8½", 9")

2" (2", 2", 2", 2", 2")

2" (2", 2", 2", 2", 2")

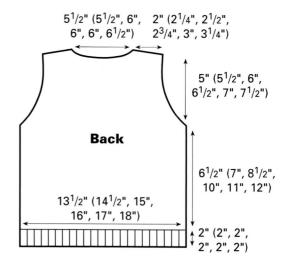

5½" (5½", 6", 6", 6", 6½")

2" (2¼", 2½", 2¾", 3", 3¼")

5" (5½", 6", 6½", 7", 7½")

Back

6½" (7", 8½", 10", 11", 12")

13½" (14½", 15", 16", 17", 18")

2" (2", 2", 2", 2", 2")

These measurements for child's sweater sizes are approximate.

Materials:

Fine (sport weight) yarn, 2½, (5, 7½, 7½, 7½, 10, 10) oz, [168 (336, 504, 504, 504, 672, 672) yds, 70 (140, 210, 210, 210, 280, 280) gms] yellow
Note: *Our photographed sweaters were made with Lion Brand Micro Spun, Buttercup #158.*
Size 8 (5mm) straight knitting needles, or size required for gauge
Size 5 (3.75mm) straight knitting needles
Size 5 (3.75mm) circular knitting needle
Size 18 tapestry needle
Four (6, 6, 6, 7, 7, 8) buttons, ½"-diameter

Gauge:
With larger size needles in stockinette stitch (knit one row, purl one row):
5 sts = 1"

Special Abbreviations

Make 1 (M1):
Insert left needle from front to back under horizontal strand between the last stitch worked and the next stitch on the left needle; knit this strand through the back loop—M1 made.

Slip, Slip, Knit (SSK):
Slip next 2 sts one at a time from the left needle to the right needle, insert the left needle into the fronts of these two stitches and knit them together—SSK made.

Instructions

Back
With smaller size needles, cast on 32 (62, 66, 68, 72, 78, 82) sts.

Ribbing:
Row 1: * K1, P1; rep from * across.
Rows 2 through 7 (15, 15, 15, 15, 15, 15):
Rep Row 1.

Next Row: Continuing in pattern as established, work 4 (6, 6, 6, 4, 8, 6) sts, M1 (see Special Abbreviations); * work 8 (10, 11, 8, 9, 9, 10) sts, M1; rep from * 2 (4, 4, 6, 6, 6, 6) times more; work 4 (6, 5, 6, 5, 7, 6) sts—36 (68, 72, 76, 80, 86, 90) sts.

Change to larger size needles.

Body:
Row 1 (right side): Knit.

Row 2: Purl.

Rep Rows 1 and 2 until piece measures about 3" (8½" 9", 10½", 12", 13", 14") from cast-on edge, ending by working a wrong side row.

Armhole Shaping:
Row 1 (right side): Bind off 3 (5, 5, 5, 6, 7, 7) sts; knit across.

Row 2: Bind off 3 (5, 5, 5, 6, 7, 7) sts; purl across—30 (58, 62, 66, 68, 72, 76) sts.

Row 3: K2, SSK (see Special Abbreviations); knit to last 4 sts; K2 tog; K2—28 (56, 60, 64, 66, 70, 74) sts.

Row 4: Purl.

Rows 5 through 6 (12, 12, 12, 12, 14, 14):
Rep Rows 3 and 4 once (4, 4, 4, 4, 5, 5) times more. At end of last row—26 (48, 52, 56, 58, 60, 64) sts.

Next Row: Knit.

Next Row: Purl.

Rep last 2 rows until piece measures about 6" (13½", 14½", 16½", 18½", 20", 21½") from cast-on edge, ending by working a wrong side row.

Shoulder Shaping:
Row 1 (right side): Bind off 2 (3, 4, 4, 4, 5, 5) sts; knit across.

Row 2: Bind off 2 (3, 4, 4, 4, 5, 5) sts; purl across—22 (42, 44, 48, 50, 50, 54) sts.

Row 3: Bind off 3 (4, 4, 5, 5, 5); knit across.

Row 4: Bind off 3 (4, 4, 5, 5, 5); purl across—16 (36, 36, 40, 40, 40, 44) sts.

For Doll Size Only:
Bind off.

Continue with Left Front on page 10.

For Sizes 2, 4, 6, 8, 10 and 12 Only:
Row 5: Bind off 4 (4, 5, 5, 5, 6) sts; knit across.
Row 6: Bind off 4 (4, 5, 5, 5, 6) sts; purl across—28 (28, 30, 30, 30, 32) sts.
Bind off.
Continue with Left Front.

Left Front
With smaller size needles, cast on 16, (31, 33, 34, 36, 39, 41) sts.

Ribbing:

For Doll Size and Sizes 6 and 8 Only:
Row 1: * K1, P1; rep from * across.
Rows 2 through 7 (15, 15): Rep Row 1.
Continue with For All Sizes below.

For Sizes 2, 4, 10 and 12 Only:
Row 1: K1; * P1, K1; rep from * across.
Row 2: P1; * K1, P1; rep from * across.
Rows 3 through 14: Rep Rows 1 and 2 six times more.
Row 15: Rep Row 1.
Continue with For All Sizes.

For All Sizes:
Next Row: Continuing in pattern as established, work 4 (8, 6, 5, 5, 6, 6) sts, M1 (see Special Abbreviations); * work 8 (8, 11, 8, 9, 9, 10), M1; rep from * 0 (1, 1, 2, 2, 2, 2) time(s) more; K4 (7, 5, 5, 4, 6, 4)—18 (34, 36, 38, 40, 43, 45) sts.
Change to larger size needles.

Body:
Row 1 (right side): Knit.
Row 2: Purl.
Rep Rows 1 and 2 until piece measures about 3", (8½", 9", 10½", 12", 13", 14") from cast-on edge, ending by working a wrong side row.

Armhole Shaping:
Row 1 (right side): Bind off 3 (5, 5, 5, 6, 7, 7) sts; knit across—15 (29, 31, 33, 34, 36, 38) sts.
Row 2: Purl.
Row 3: K2, SSK (see Special Abbreviations); knit across—14 (28, 30, 32, 33, 35, 37) sts.
Row 4: Purl.
Rows 5 through 6 (12, 12, 12, 12, 14, 14): Rep Rows 3 and 4 once (4, 4, 4, 4, 5, 5) times more. At end of last row—13 (24, 26, 28, 29, 30, 32) sts.
Next Row: Knit.

Next Row: Purl.
Rep last 2 rows until piece measures about 4½", (11", 11¾", 13½", 15½", 17", 19½") from cast-on edge, ending by working a wrong side row.

Neck Shaping:
Row 1 (right side): Knit.
Row 2: Bind off 4 (8, 8, 9, 9, 8, 9) sts; purl across—9 (16, 18, 19, 20, 22, 23) sts.
Row 3: Knit to last 4 sts; K2 tog; K2—8 (15, 17, 18, 19, 21, 22) sts.
Row 4: Purl.
Rows 5 through 10 (14, 14, 14, 14, 16, 16): Rep Rows 3 and 4 three (5, 5, 5, 5, 6, 6) times more. At end of last row—5 (10, 12, 13, 14, 15, 16) sts.
Next Row: Knit.
Next Row: Purl.
Rep last 2 rows until piece measures about 6" (13½", 14½", 16½", 18½", 20", 21½") from cast-on edge, ending by working a wrong side row.

Shoulder Shaping:
Row 1: Bind off 2 (3, 4, 4, 4, 5, 5) sts; knit across—3 (7, 8, 9, 10, 10, 11) sts.
Row 2: Purl.

For Doll Size Only:
Bind off.
Continue with Right Front below.

For Sizes 2, 4, 6, 8, 10 and 12 Only:
Row 3: Bind off 3 (4, 4, 5, 5, 5) sts; knit across—4 (4, 5, 5, 5, 6) sts.
Row 4: Purl.
Row 5: Bind off.

Right Front
Work same as Left Front to Armhole Shaping.

Armhole Shaping:
Row 1 (right side): Knit.
Row 2: Bind off 3 (5, 5, 5, 6, 7, 7) sts; purl across—15 (29, 31, 33, 34, 36, 38) sts.
Row 3: Knit to last 4 sts; K2 tog; K2—14 (28, 30, 32, 33, 35, 37) sts.
Row 4: Purl.
Rows 5 through 6 (12, 12, 12, 12, 14, 14): Rep Rows 3 and 4 once (4, 4, 4, 4, 5, 5) times more. At end of last row—13 (24, 26, 28, 29, 30, 32) sts.
Next Row: Knit.
Next Row: Purl.

Rep last 2 rows until piece measures about 4½" (11", 11¾", 13½", 15½", 17", 19½") from cast-on edge, ending by working a wrong side row.

Neck Shaping:
Row 1 (right side): Bind off 4 (8, 8, 9, 9, 8, 9) sts; knit across—9 (16, 18, 19, 20, 22, 23) sts.

Row 2: Purl.

Row 3: K2, SSK (see Special Abbreviations); knit across.

Row 4: Purl.

Rows 5 through 10 (14, 14, 14, 14, 16, 16): Rep Rows 3 and 4 three (5, 5, 5, 5, 6, 6) times more. At end of last row—5 (10, 12, 13, 14, 15, 16) sts.

Next Row: Knit.

Next Row: Purl.

Rep last 2 rows until piece measures about 6" (13½", 14½", 16½", 18½", 20", 21½") from cast-on edge, ending by working a wrong side row.

Shoulder Shaping:
Row 1 (right side): Knit.

Row 2: Bind off 2 (3, 4, 4, 4, 5, 5) sts; purl across.

Row 3: Knit.

For Doll Size Only:
Bind off.

Continue with Assembly below.

For Sizes 2, 4, 6, 8, 10 and 12 Only:
Row 4: Bind off 3 (4, 4, 5, 5, 5) sts; purl across.

Row 5: Knit.

Bind off.

Assembly
Sew shoulder and side seams.

Edgings

Armhole Edging:
With circular needle, pick up 36 (60, 66, 70, 76, 80, 86) sts along armhole edge.

Rnd 1: * K1, P1; rep from * around.

Rep Rnd 1 until ribbing measures ¾".

Bind off loosely in ribbing.

Rep for other armhole.

Neck Edging:
Hold piece with right side facing you and neck edge at top; with smaller size needles pick up 17 (19, 21, 24, 24, 24, 24) sts evenly spaced along right front neck edge; 16 (28, 28, 30, 30, 30, 32) sts across back neck edge; 17 (19, 21, 24, 24, 24, 24) evenly spaced along left front neck edge—50 (60, 70, 78, 78, 78, 80) sts.

Row 1: * K1, P1; rep from * across.

Rep Row 1 until ribbing measures about 1¼" (2", 2", 2", 2", 2", 2").

Bind off loosely in ribbing.

Right Front Edging (button band):
Hold piece with right side of right front facing you; with smaller size needles pick up 34 (72, 76, 84, 96, 104, 118) sts along center front edge.

Row 1 (wrong side): * K1, P1; rep from * across.

Rep Row 1 until ribbing measures about ½" (1", 1", 1", 1", 1", 1").

Bind off loosely in ribbing.

Left Front Edging (buttonhole band):
Hold piece with left side of right front facing you; with smaller size needles pick up 34 (72, 76, 84, 96, 104, 118) sts along center front edge.

For Doll Size Only:
Row 1: * K1, P1; rep from * across.

Row 2: Continuing in rib pattern as established, K1, P1; bind off 2 sts; * work next 7 sts, bind off 2 sts; rep from * twice more; work next 3 sts.

Row 3: * Work in pattern to bound off sts; cast on 2 sts; rep from * 3 times more; work rem sts.

Row 4: * K1, P1; rep from * across.

Bind off loosely in ribbing.

Continue with Finishing.

For Sizes 2, 4, 6, 8, 10 and 12 Only:
Row 1: * K1, P1; rep from * across.

Rows 2 and 3: Rep Row 1.

Row 4: Continuing in rib pattern as established, work 5 (5, 6, 5, 6, 6) sts; bind off 2 sts; * work 10 (11, 12, 12, 13, 13) sts, bind off 2 sts; rep from * 4 (4, 4, 5, 5, 6) times more; work 5 (4, 6, 5, 6, 5) sts.

Row 5: * Work in pattern to bound off sts; cast on 2 sts; rep from * 5 (5, 5, 6, 6, 7) times more; work rem sts.

Rows 6 and 7: Rep Row 1.

Bind off loosely in ribbing.

Continue with Finishing.

Finishing
Sew buttons opposite buttonholes.

Keen Cardigan

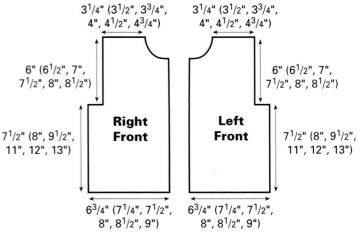

■■■□ INTERMEDIATE

Sizes:

18" doll	2	4	6	8	10	12

Finished Chest Size:

14"	27"	28½"	30"	32"	34"	36"

Note: *Instructions are written for doll; changes for other sizes are in parentheses.*

Right Front / Left Front:

3$\frac{1}{4}$" (3$\frac{1}{2}$", 3$\frac{3}{4}$", 4", 4$\frac{1}{2}$", 4$\frac{3}{4}$")

6" (6$\frac{1}{2}$", 7", 7$\frac{1}{2}$", 8", 8$\frac{1}{2}$")

7$\frac{1}{2}$" (8", 9$\frac{1}{2}$", 11", 12", 13")

6$\frac{3}{4}$" (7$\frac{1}{4}$", 7$\frac{1}{2}$", 8", 8$\frac{1}{2}$", 9")

Back:

12" (12$\frac{1}{2}$", 13", 14", 15", 16")

6" (6$\frac{1}{2}$", 7", 7$\frac{1}{2}$", 8", 8$\frac{1}{2}$")

7$\frac{1}{2}$" (8", 9$\frac{1}{2}$", 11", 12", 13")

13$\frac{1}{2}$" (14", 15", 16", 17", 18")

Sleeve:

12" (13", 14", 15", 16", 17")

8$\frac{1}{2}$" (9$\frac{1}{2}$", 11$\frac{1}{4}$", 12$\frac{3}{4}$", 14$\frac{1}{4}$", 15")

6" (6$\frac{3}{4}$", 7", 7$\frac{1}{2}$", 7$\frac{1}{2}$", 7$\frac{1}{2}$")

2" (2", 2", 2", 2", 2")

These measurements for child's sweater sizes are approximate.

Materials:

Fine (sport weight) yarn, 2½ (7½, 7½ 10, 12½, 12½, 15) oz [168 (504, 504, 672, 840, 840, 1008) yds, 70 (210, 210, 280, 350, 350, 420) gms] blue; 2½ oz (168 yds, 70 gms) green (for all sizes)

Note: *Our photographed sweater was made with Lion Brand Micro Spun, Royal Blue #109 and Lime #194.*

Size 8 (5mm) straight knitting needles, or size required for gauge
Size 5 (3.75mm) straight knitting needles
Size 5 (3.75mm) circular knitting needle (for neck)
Size 18 tapestry needle
Four (5, 5, 5, 6, 6, 6) buttons, ⅝"-diameter

Gauge:

With larger size needles in stockinette stitch (knit one row, purl one row):
5 sts = 1"

Special Abbreviations

Make 1 (M1):
Insert left needle from front to back under horizontal strand between the last stitch worked and the next stitch on the left needle; knit this strand through the back loop—M1 made.

Slip, Slip, Knit (SSK):
Slip next 2 sts one at a time from the left needle to the right needle, insert the left needle into the fronts of these two stitches and knit them together—SSK made.

Instructions

Back
With smaller size straight needles and green, cast on 32 (62, 66, 68, 72, 78, 82) sts.

Edging:
Row 1: Knit.

Rows 2 through 6 (8, 8, 8, 8, 8, 8): Rep Row 1.

Next Row: K4 (6, 6, 6, 4, 8, 6), M1 (see Special Abbreviations); * K8 (10, 11, 8, 9, 9, 10), M1; rep from * 2 (4, 4, 6, 6, 6,6) times more; K4 (6, 5, 6, 5, 7, 6)—36 (68, 72, 76, 80, 86, 90) sts.

Change to larger size needles and blue.

Body:
Row 1 (right side): Knit.

Row 2: Purl.

Rep Rows 1 and 2 until piece measures about 2¾" (7½", 8", 9½", 11", 12", 13") from cast-on edge, ending by working a wrong side row.

Armhole Shaping:
Row 1 (right side): Bind off 2 (4, 5, 5, 5, 5, 5) sts; knit across.

Row 2: Bind off 2 (4, 5, 5, 5, 5, 5) sts; purl across—32 (60, 62, 66, 70, 76, 80) sts.

Row 3: Knit.

Row 4: Purl.

Rep Rows 3 and 4 until piece measures about 5¾" (13½", 14½", 16½", 18½", 20", 21½") from cast-on edge, ending by working a wrong side row.

Bind off.

Left Front

With smaller size straight needles and green, cast on 16 (31, 33, 34, 36, 39, 41) sts.

Edging:
Row 1: Knit.

Rows 2 through 6 (8, 8, 8, 8, 8, 8): Rep Row 1.

Next Row: K4 (8, 6, 5, 5, 6, 6), M1 (see Special Abbreviations on page 13); * K8 (8, 11, 8, 9, 9, 10), M1; rep from * 0 (1, 1, 2, 2, 2, 2) times more; K4 (7, 5, 5, 4, 6, 4)—18 (34, 36, 38, 40, 43, 45) sts.

Change to larger size needles and blue.

Body:
Row 1 (right side): Knit.

Row 2: Purl.

Rep Rows 1 and 2 until piece measures about 2¾" (7½", 8", 9½", 11", 12", 13") from cast-on edge, ending by working a wrong side row.

Armhole Shaping:
Row 1 (right side): Bind off 2 (4, 5, 5, 5, 5, 5) sts; knit across—16 (30, 31, 33, 35, 38, 40) sts.

Row 2: Purl.

Row 3: Knit.

Row 4: Purl.

Rep Rows 3 and 4 until piece measures about 4¼" (11", 11¾", 13½", 15½", 17", 18½") from cast-on edge, ending by working a wrong side row.

Neck Shaping:
Row 1 (right side): Knit.

Row 2: Bind off 4 (7, 7, 8, 8, 8, 8) sts; purl across—12 (23, 24, 25, 28, 30, 32) sts.

Row 3: Knit to last 4 sts; K2 tog; K2—11 (22, 23, 24, 27, 29, 31) sts.

Row 4: Purl.

Rows 5 through 10 (16, 16, 16, 16, 16, 18): Rep Rows 3 and 4 three (6, 6, 6, 6, 6, 7) times more. At end of last row—8 (16, 17, 18, 20, 23, 24) sts.

Next Row: Knit.

Next Row: Purl.

Rep last 2 rows until piece measures about 5¾" (13½", 14½", 16½", 18½", 20", 21½") from cast-on edge, ending by working a wrong side row.

Bind off.

Right Front

With smaller size needles and green, cast on 16 (31, 33, 34, 36, 39, 41) sts.

Edging:
Row 1: Knit.

Rows 2 through 6 (8, 8, 8, 8, 8, 8): Rep Row 1.

Next Row: K4 (8, 6, 5, 5, 6, 6), M1 (see Special Abbreviations on page 13); * K8 (8, 11, 8, 9, 9, 10), M1; rep from * 0 (1, 1, 2, 2, 2, 2) times more; K4 (7, 5, 5, 4, 6, 4)—18 (34, 36, 38, 40, 43, 45) sts.

Change to larger size needles and blue.

Body:
Row 1 (right side): Knit.

Row 2: Purl.

Rep Rows 1 and 2 until piece measures about 2¾" (7½", 8", 9½", 11", 12", 13") from cast-on edge, ending by working a wrong side row.

Armhole Shaping:
Row 1 (right side): Knit.

Row 2: Bind off 2 (4, 5, 5, 5, 5, 5) sts; purl across—16 (30, 31, 33, 35, 38, 40) sts.

Row 3: Knit.

Row 4: Purl.

Rep Rows 3 and 4 until piece measures about 4¼" (11", 11¾", 13½", 15½", 17", 18½") from cast-on edge, ending by working a wrong side row.

Neck Shaping:
Row 1 (right side): Bind off 4 (7, 7, 8, 8, 8, 8) sts; knit across—12 (23, 24, 25, 28, 30, 32) sts.

Row 2: Purl.

Row 3: K2, SSK (see Special Abbreviations on page 13); knit across—11 (22, 23, 24, 27, 29, 31) sts.

Row 4: Purl.

Rows 5 through 10 (16, 16, 16, 16, 16, 18): Rep Rows 3 and 4 three (5, 5, 5, 5, 5, 6) times more. At end of last row—8 (16, 17, 18, 20, 23, 24) sts.

Next Row: Knit.

Next Row: Purl.

Rep last 2 rows until piece measures about 5¾" (13½", 14½", 16½", 18½", 20", 21½") from cast-on edge, ending by working a wrong side row.

Bind off.

Sew shoulder seams.

Sleeve

Hold piece with right side of one armhole edge facing you; with smaller size straight needles and blue, pick up 30 (60, 66, 70, 76, 80, 86) sts along armhole edge beginning and ending above bound off sts of armhole shaping and having same number of sts on front and back.

Change to larger size needles.

Row 1 (wrong side): Purl.

Row 2 (right side): Knit.

Row 3: Purl.

Row 4: K2, SSK (see Special Abbreviations on page 13), knit to last 4 sts; K2 tog; K2—28 (58, 64, 68, 74, 78, 84) sts.

Row 5: Purl.

Rows 6 through 17 (49, 57, 61, 69, 77, 89): Rep Rows 2 through 5 three (11, 13, 14, 16, 18, 21) times more. At end of last row—22 (36, 38, 40, 42, 42, 42) sts.

Rep Rows 2 and 3 until sleeve measures about 3¾" (8½", 9½", 11¼", 12¾", 14¼", 15"), ending by working a right side row.

Next Row: P6 (4, 5, 4, 5, 5, 5), P2 tog; * P6 (7, 7, 8, 8, 8, 8), P2 tog; rep from * 0 (3, 3, 3, 3, 3, 3) times more; P6 (3, 4, 4, 5, 5, 5)—20 (32, 34, 36, 38, 38, 38) sts.

Change to smaller size straight needles and green.

Edging:

Row 1 (right side): Knit.

Rows 2 through 5 (9, 9, 9, 9, 9, 9): Rep Row 1.
Bind off.
Rep for other sleeve.

Edgings

Neck Edging:

Hold piece with right side facing you and neck edge at top; with smaller size circular needle and green pick up 15 (24, 27, 29, 29, 29, 29) sts along right front neck edge; 16 (28, 27, 30, 30, 30, 32) sts across back neck edge; 15 (24, 27, 29, 29, 29, 29) sts along left front neck edge—46 (76, 82, 88, 88, 88, 90) sts.

Row 1: Knit.

Rows 2 through 7: Rep Row 1.
Bind off.

Left Front Edging (button band):

Hold piece with right side of left front facing you; with smaller size needles and green pick up 27 (66, 70, 78, 86, 96, 106) sts along center front edge.

Row 1: Knit.

Rows 2 through 6 (8, 8, 8, 8, 8, 8): Rep Row 1.
Bind off.

Right Front Edging (buttonhole band):

Hold piece with right side of right front facing you; with smaller size needles and green pick up 27 (66, 70, 78, 86, 96, 106) sts along center front edge.

For Doll Size Only:

Row 1: Knit.

Row 2: Rep Row 1.

Row 3: K2, bind off 2 sts; * K5, bind off 2 sts; rep from * twice more; knit across.

Row 4: * Knit to bound off sts; cast on 2 sts; rep from * twice more; knit across.

Rows 5 and 6: Rep Row 1.
Bind off.
Continue with Finishing below.

Row Sizes 2, 4, 6, 8, 10 and 12 Only:

Row 1: Knit.

Rows 2 and 3: Rep Row 1.

Row 4: K2, bind off 2 sts; * K13 (14, 16, 14, 16, 18), bind off 2 sts; rep from * 3 (3, 3, 4, 4, 4) times more; knit across.

Row 5: * Knit to bound off sts; cast on 2 sts; rep from * 3 (3, 3, 4, 4, 4) times more; knit across.

Rows 6 through 8: Rep Row 1.
Bind off.
Continue with Finishing.

Finishing

Step 1: Sew side edges at top of sleeve to bound off sts of front and back armholes.

Step 2: Sew sleeve and side seams.

Step 3: Sew buttons on left front band under buttonholes.

Happy Day Hooded Cardigan

◼◼◼◻ INTERMEDIATE

Sizes:

18" doll	2	4	6	8	10	12

Finished Chest Size:

14"	27"	28½"	30"	32"	34"	37"

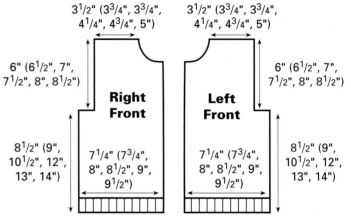

3¹/₂" (3³/₄", 3³/₄", 4¹/₄", 4³/₄", 5")   3¹/₂" (3³/₄", 3³/₄", 4¹/₄", 4³/₄", 5")

6" (6¹/₂", 7", 7¹/₂", 8", 8¹/₂")

Right Front   **Left Front**

6" (6¹/₂", 7", 7¹/₂", 8", 8¹/₂")

8¹/₂" (9", 10¹/₂", 12", 13", 14")

7¹/₄" (7³/₄", 8", 8¹/₂", 9", 9¹/₂")   7¹/₄" (7³/₄", 8", 8¹/₂", 9", 9¹/₂")

8¹/₂" (9", 10¹/₂", 12", 13", 14")

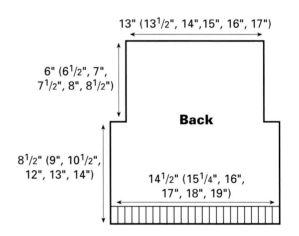

13" (13¹/₂", 14", 15", 16", 17")

6" (6¹/₂", 7", 7¹/₂", 8", 8¹/₂")

Back

8¹/₂" (9", 10¹/₂", 12", 13", 14")

14¹/₂" (15¹/₄", 16", 17", 18", 19")

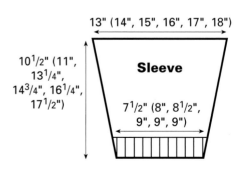

13" (14", 15", 16", 17", 18")

10¹/₂" (11", 13¹/₄", 14³/₄", 16¹/₄", 17¹/₂")

Sleeve

7¹/₂" (8", 8¹/₂", 9", 9", 9")

These measurements for child's sweater sizes are approximate.

Materials:

Light (worsted weight) yarn, 5 (15, 15, 20, 20, 25, 25) oz [236 (708, 708, 944, 944, 1180, 1180) yds, 142 (426, 426, 568, 568, 710, 710) gms] green
Note: Our photographed sweaters were made with Lion Brand Cotton-Ease Pistachio #169.
Size 8 (5mm) straight knitting needles, or size required for gauge
Size 5 (3.75mm) straight knitting needles
Small safety pin (for stitch marker)
Size 18 tapestry needle
Three (5, 5, 5, 5, 5) buttons, ⅝"-diameter

Gauge:

With larger size needles in stockinette stitch (knit one row, purl one row):
4 sts = 1"

Special Abbreviations

Make 1 (M1):
Insert left needle from front to back under horizontal strand between the last stitch worked and the next stitch on the left needle; knit this strand through the back loop—M1 made.

Make 1 with right twist (M1R):
Insert left needle from back to front under horizontal strand between last stitch worked and the next stitch on the left needle; knit this strand through the front loop—M1R made.

Slip, Slip, Knit (SSK):
Slip next 2 sts one at a time from the left needle to the right needle, insert the left needle into the fronts of these two stitches and knit them together—SSK made.

Instructions

Back
With smaller size needles, cast on 28 (52, 56, 58, 62, 66, 68) sts.

Ribbing:
Row 1 (right side): * K1, P1; rep from * across.

Rows 2 through 5 (11, 11, 11, 11, 11, 11): Rep Row 1.

Next Row: P7 (6, 6, 7, 6, 6, 5), M1 (see Special Abbreviations); * P17 (8, 9, 9, 10, 11, 9), M1; rep from * 0 (4, 4, 4, 4, 4, 6) times more; P7 (6, 5, 6, 6, 5, 4)—30 (58, 62, 64, 68, 72, 76) sts.

Change to larger size needles.

Body:
Row 1 (right side): Knit.

Row 2: Purl.

Rep Rows 1 and 2 until piece measures about 3" (8½", 9", 10½", 12", 13", 14") from cast-on edge, ending by working a wrong side row.

Armhole Shaping:
Row 1 (right side): Bind off 1 (3, 4, 4, 4, 4, 4) sts; knit across.

Row 2: Bind off 1 (3, 4, 4, 4, 4, 4) sts; purl across—28 (52, 54, 56, 60, 64, 68) sts.

Row 3: Knit.

Row 4: Purl.

Rep Rows 3 and 4 until piece measures about 6" (14", 15½", 17½", 19½", 21", 23") from cast-on edge, ending by working a wrong side row.

Bind off.

Left Front

With smaller size needles, cast on 14 (26, 28, 29, 31, 33, 34) sts.

Ribbing:

For Doll Size Only:

Row 1 (right side): * K1, P1; rep from * across.

Rows 2 through 5: Rep Row 1.

Row 6: P7, M1; P7—15 sts.

Change to larger size needles.

Continue with Body below.

For Sizes 2, 4 and 12 Only:

Row 1 (right side): K1, P1; rep from * across.

Rows 2 through 11: Rep Row 1.

Row 12: P5, M1; * P8 (9, 9), M1; rep from * once (once, twice) more —29 (31, 38) sts.

Change to larger size needles.

Continue with Body below.

For Sizes 6, 8, and 10 Only:

Row 1 (right side): K1; * P1, K1; rep from * across.

Row 2: P1; * K1, P1; rep from * across.

Rows 3 through 10: Rep Rows 1 and 2 four times more.

Row 11: Rep Row 1.

Row 12: P6, M1; * P9 (10, 11), M1; rep from * once more—32 (34, 36) sts.

Change to larger size needles.

Continue with Body.

Body:

Row 1 (right side): Knit.

Row 2: Purl.

Rep Rows 1 and 2 until piece measures about 3" (8½", 9", 10½", 12", 13", 14") from cast-on edge, ending by working a wrong side row.

Armhole Shaping:

Row 1 (right side): Bind off 1 (3, 4, 4, 4, 4, 4) st(s); knit across.

Row 2: Purl.

Row 3: Knit.

Rep Rows 2 and 3 until piece measures 4½" (12, 12¾", 14½", 16½", 18", 19½") from cast-on edge, ending by working a right side row.

Neck Shaping:

Row 1 (wrong side): Bind off 4 (6, 6, 7, 7, 7, 8) sts; purl across.

Row 2 (right side): Knit to last 3 sts; K2 tog; K1.

Row 3: Purl.

Rows 4 through 7 (13, 13, 13, 13, 15, 13): Rep Rows 2 and 3 two (5, 5, 5, 5, 6, 5) times more. At end of Row last row—7 (14, 15, 15, 17, 19, 20) sts.

Row 8: Knit.

Row 9: Purl.

Rep Rows 8 and 9 until piece measures about 6" (14½", 15½", 17½", 19½", 21", 23") from cast-on edge, ending by working a wrong side row.

Bind off.

Right Front

Work same as Left Front to Armhole Shaping.

Armhole Shaping:

Row 1 (right side): Knit.

Row 2: Bind off 1 (3, 4, 4, 4, 4, 4) st(s); purl across.

Row 3: Knit.

Row 4: Purl.

Rep Rows 3 and 4 until piece measures 4½" (12" (12¾", 14½", 16½". 18", 19½") ending by working a wrong side row.

Neck Shaping:

Row 1 (right side): Bind off 4 (6, 6, 7, 7, 7, 8) sts; knit across.

Row 2: Purl.

Row 3: K1, SSK (see Special Abbreviations on page 17); knit across.

Row 4: Purl.

Rows 5 through 8 (14, 14, 14, 14, 16, 14): Rep Rows 3 and 4 two (5, 5, 5, 5, 6, 5) times more. At end of last row—7 (14, 15, 15, 17, 19, 20) sts.

Row 9: Knit.

Row 10: Purl.

Rep Rows 9 and 10 until piece measures about 6" (14½", 15½", 17½", 19½", 21", 22½") from cast-on edge, ending by working a wrong side row.

Bind off.

Sleeves (make 2)

With smaller size needles, cast on 16 (28, 30, 32, 32, 32, 32) sts.

Ribbing:

Row 1 (right side): K1, P1; rep from * across.

Rows 2 through 5 (11, 11, 11, 11, 11, 11): Rep Row 1.

For Doll Size Only:

Row 6: P4, M1 (see Special Abbreviations on page 17); P8, M1; P4—18 sts.

Change to larger size needles.

Continue with Body below.

For Sizes 2, 4, 6, 8, 10 and 12 Only:

Row 12: P7 (8, 8, 4, 4, 4), M1 (see Special Abbreviations on page 17); * P14 (15, 16, 8, 8, 8), M1; rep from * 0 (0, 0, 2, 2, 2) times more; P7 (5, 5, 5, 5, 4)—30 (32, 34, 36, 36, 36) sts.

Change to larger size needles.

Continue with Body.

Body:

Row 1 (right side): Knit.

Row 2: Purl.

Row 3: K2, M1; knit to last 2 sts; M1R (see Special Abbreviations on page 17); K2—20 (32, 34, 36, 38, 38, 38) sts.

Row 4: Purl.

Rows 5 through 16 (44, 48, 52, 56, 64, 72): Rep Rows 1 through 4 three (10, 11, 12, 13, 15, 17) times more. At end of last row—26, (52, 56, 60, 64, 68, 72) sts.

Next Row: Knit.

Next Row: Purl.

Rep last 2 rows until piece measures about 4½" (10½", 11", 13¼", 14¾", 16¼", 17½") from cast-on edge, ending by working a wrong side row.

Bind off.

Assembly

Sew shoulder seams. Sew sleeves to front and back beginning and ending above bound off armhole stitches and having center of bound off edge of sleeve at shoulder seam. Sew sleeve and side seams.

Bands

Right Front Band (button band):
Hold sweater with right side of right front facing you and center front edge at top; with smaller size needles, pick up 26 (62, 66, 74, 82, 90, 102) sts evenly spaced along center front edge.

Row 1 (wrong side): K1, P1; rep from * across.

Rows 2 (right side) **through 4 (6, 6, 6, 6, 6):** Rep Row 1.

Bind off loosely in ribbing.

Left Front Band (buttonhole band):
Hold sweater with right side of left front facing you and center front at edge at top, with smaller size needles pick up 26 (62, 66, 74, 82, 90, 102) sts evenly spaced along center front edge.

For Doll Size Only:

Row 1 (wrong side): * K1, P1; rep from * across.

Row 2 (right side): K1, P1, bind off next 2 sts; * work next 8 sts in pattern, bind off next 2 sts; rep from * twice more; work in pattern across.

Row 3: * Work in pattern to bound off sts, cast on 2 sts; rep from * twice more; work in pattern across.

Row 4: Rep Row 1.

Bind off in ribbing.

Continue with Hood below.

For Sizes 2, 4, 6, 8, 10 and 12 Only:

Row 1 (wrong side): * K1, P1; rep from * across.

Rows 2 and 3: Rep Row 1.

Row 4 (right side): K1, P1, bind off next 2 sts, * work next 12 (13, 15, 17, 19, 22) sts in pattern, bind off next 2 sts; rep from * 3 times more; work in pattern across.

Row 5: * Work in pattern as established to bound off sts, cast on 2 sts; rep from * 3 times more; work in pattern across.

Rows 6 and 7: Rep Row 1.

Bind off loosely in pattern.

Continue with Hood.

Hood

Hold sweater with right side facing you and right front neck edge at top, with smaller size needles pick up 4 (6, 6, 7, 7, 7, 7) sts in bound off sts of right front neck edge; working along neck edge in ends of rows, pick up 10 (14, 16, 17, 17, 16, 16) sts evenly spaced to shoulder seam; working across back, pick up 7 (12, 12, 13, 13, 13, 14) sts evenly spaced to center back; place marker on needle; pick up 7 (12, 12, 13, 13, 13, 14) sts evenly spaced to left shoulder seam; working along left front neck edge in ends of rows, pick up 10 (14, 16, 17, 17, 16, 16) sts evenly spaced to bound off sts; pick up 4 (6, 6, 7, 7, 7, 7) sts in bound off sts of left front neck edge—42 (64, 68, 74, 74, 72, 74) sts.

Row 1 (wrong side): K4 (6, 6, 6, 6, 6, 6) purl to last 4 (6, 6, 6, 6, 6, 6) sts; K4 (6, 6, 6, 6, 6, 6).

Row 2 (right side): Knit.

Row 3: K4 (6, 6, 6, 6, 6, 6) purl to last 4 (6, 6, 6, 6, 6, 6) sts; K4 (6, 6, 6, 6, 6, 6).

Rep Rows 2 and 3 until hood measures about 1½", (2½", 2¾", 3", 3", 3", 3"), ending by working a wrong side row.

Hood Increases:

For Doll Size Only:

Row 1 (right side): Knit to one stitch before marker, M1; K2, M1R (see Special Abbreviations on page 17); knit across.

Row 2: K4, purl to last 4 sts; K4.

Row 3: Knit.

Row 4: Rep Row 2.

Rows 5 through 36: Rep Rows 1 through 4 eight times more. At end of Row 36—60 sts.

Continue with For All Sizes.

For Sizes 2 and 4 Only:

Row 1 (right side): Knit to one stitch before marker, M1; K2, M1R (see Special Abbreviations on page 17); knit across.

Row 2: K6, purl to last 6 sts; K6.

Row 3: Knit.

Row 4: Rep Row 2.

Rows 5 through 8: Rep Rows 3 and 4 twice more.

Rows 9 through 48: Rep Rows 1 through 8 five times more. At end of Row 48—76 (80) sts.

Continue with For All Sizes.

For Sizes 6 and 8 Only:

Row 1 (right side): Knit to one stitch before marker, M1; K2, M1R (see Special Abbreviations on page 17); knit across.

Row 2: K6, purl to last 6 sts; K6.

Row 3: Knit.

Row 4: Rep Row 2.

Rows 5 through 10: Rep Rows 3 and 4 three times.

Rows 11 through 50: Rep Rows 1 through 10 four times more. At end of Row 50—84 (84) sts.

Continue with For All Sizes.

For Size 10 Only:

Row 1 (right side): Knit to one stitch before marker, M1; K2, M1R (see Special Abbreviations on page 17); knit across.

Row 2: K6, purl to last 6 sts; K6.

Row 3: Knit.

Row 4: Rep Row 2.

Rows 5 and 6: Rep Rows 3 and 4.

Rows 7 through 48: Rep Rows 1 through 6 seven times more. At end of Row 48—84 sts.

Continue with For All Sizes below.

For Size 12 Only:

Row 1 (right side): Knit to one stitch before marker, M1; K2, M1R (see Special Abbreviations on page 17); knit across.

Row 2: K6, purl to last 6 sts; K6.

Row 3: Knit.

Row 4: Rep Row 2.

Rows 5 through 24: Rep Rows 1 through 4 five times more. At end of Row 24—84 sts.

Row 25: Knit to one stitch before marker, M1; K2, M1R; knit across.

Row 26: K6, purl to last 6 sts; K6.

Row 27: Knit.

Row 28: Rep Row 26.

Rows 29 and 30: Rep Rows 27 and 28.

Rows 31 through 54: Rep Rows 25 through 30 four times more. At end of Row 54—96 sts.

Continue with For All Sizes.

For All Sizes:

Next Row: Knit.

Next Row: K4 (6, 6, 6, 6, 6, 6) purl to last 4 (6, 6, 6, 6, 6, 6) sts; K4 (6, 6, 6, 6, 6, 6).

Rep last two rows until hood measures about 7½" (10½", 10¾", 12", 12½", 12¼", 13") ending by working a wrong side row.

Bind off.

Finishing

Step 1: Fold last row of hood in half. Sew hood seam.

Step 2: Sew buttons to right front band under buttonholes.

Pretty Pink Tunic

Pretty Pink Tunic (for doll)

⬛⬛⬛▢ INTERMEDIATE

Size:
18" doll

Finished Chest Size:
14"

Materials:
Fine (sport weight) yarn, 5 oz (336 yds, 140 gms) pink
Note: *Our photographed sweater was made with Lion Brand Micro Spun, Peppermint Pink #101.*
Size 8 (5mm) straight knitting needles, or size required for gauge
Size 5 (3.75mm) double-pointed knitting needles (for neck)
Small safety pins (for markers)
Size 18 tapestry needle

Gauge:
With larger size needles in stockinette stitch (knit one row, purl one row):
5 sts = 1"

Special Abbreviations

Slip, Slip, Knit (SSK):
Slip next 2 sts one at a time from the left needle to the right needle, insert the left needle into the front of these two stitches and knit them together—SSK made.

Make 1 (M1):
Insert left needle from front to back under horizontal strand between the last stitch worked and the next stitch on the left needle; knit this strand through the back loop—M1 made.

Instructions

Back
With larger size needles, cast on 83 sts.

Ruffle Border:
Row 1 (wrong side): K3; * P5, K3; rep from * 9 times more.

Row 2 (right side): P3, * K5, P3; rep from * 9 times more.

Row 3: K3, * P5, K3; rep from * 9 times more.

Row 4: P3; * K1, sl next 2 sts as to knit, K1, P2SSO; K1, P3; rep from * across—63 sts.

Row 5: K3; * P3, K3; rep from * 9 times more.

Row 6: P3; * K3, P3; rep from * 9 times more.

Row 7: Rep Row 5.

Row 8: P3; * sl next 2 sts as to knit, K1, P2SSO; P3; rep from * across—43 sts.

Row 9: K3; * P1, K3; rep from * 9 times more.

Row 10: P3; * K1, P3; rep from * 9 times more.

Rows 11 and 12: Rep Rows 9 and 10.

Row 13: Knit.

Body:
Row 1 (wrong side): Purl.

Row 2 (right side): Knit.

Rows 3, 5, 7, 9, 11, 13 and 15: Purl.

Row 4: K5; * SSK (see Special Abbreviations); YO; K6; rep from * 3 times more; SSK; YO; K4.

Row 6: K4: * SSK; YO; K1, YO; K2 tog; K3; rep from * 3 times more; SSK, YO; K1, YO; K2 tog; K2.

Row 8: Rep Row 4.

Row 10: Knit.

Row 12: K9; * SSK; YO; K6; rep from * twice more; SSK; YO; K8.

Row 14: K8; * SSK; YO; K1, YO; K2 tog; K3; rep from * twice more; SSK; YO; K1, YO; K2 tog; K6.

Row 16: Rep Row 12.

Rep Rows 1 through 16 until piece measures about 5½" from cast-on edge, ending by working a Row 11.

Armhole:
Place marker at beginning and end of next row for armhole.

Continue in pattern until piece measures about 9" from cast-on edge.

Bind off.

Front
Work same as Back to Armhole.

Place marker at beginning and end of next row for armhole.

Continue in pattern as established until piece measures about 8" from cast-on edge, ending by working a Row 8.

Neck Shaping:
Row 1 (wrong side): For right shoulder, P15 sts; join a second skein of yarn; for neck, bind off next 13 sts; for left shoulder, purl rem sts—15 sts on each shoulder.

Note: Work both shoulders at same time with separate skeins of yarn.

Row 2 (right side): For left shoulder, work in pattern to last 3 sts; K2 tog; K1; for right shoulder, K1, SSK; work in pattern across—14 sts on each shoulder.

Row 3: Purl across both shoulders.

Rows 4 through 9: Rep Rows 2 and 3 three times more. At end of Row 9—11 sts on each shoulder.

Continue to work in pattern until piece measures 9" from cast-on edge.

Bind off.

Sleeve (make 2)
With smaller size needles, cast on 24 sts.

Border:
Row 1: Knit.

Rows 2 and 3: Rep Row 1.

Row 4: K4, M1 (see Special Abbreviations); * K6, M1; rep from * once more; K4—27 sts.

Body:
Row 1: K1, M1; K8; * SSK; YO; K6; rep from * once more; K1, M1; K1—29 sts.

Row 2 and all even rows: Purl.

Row 3: K9, SSK; YO; K1, YO; K2 tog; K3, SSK; YO; K1, YO; K2 tog; K7.

Row 5: K1, M1; K9, SSK; YO; K6, SSK; YO; K8; M1, K1—31 sts.

Row 7: Knit.

Row 9: K6; * SSK; YO; K6; rep from * twice more; K1.

Row 11: K1, M1; K4; * SSK; YO; K1, YO; K2 tog; K3; rep from twice more; K1, M1; K1—33 sts.

Row 13: K7; * SSK; YO; K6; rep from * twice more; K2.

Row 15: K1, M1; knit to last st; M1; K1—35 sts.

Continue in pattern inc one st each end every 4th row once more—37 sts.

Continue even (without inc) in pattern until sleeve measures about 4½" from cast-on edge

Bind off.

Assembly
Sew shoulder seams. Sew sleeves to front and back between markers having center of bound off edge of sleeve at shoulder seam. Sew sleeve and side seams.

Neck Edging
Hold tunic with right sides facing you and neck edge at top; beg at one shoulder seam with double-pointed needles pick up 56 sts evenly spaced around neck edge.

Row 1: Purl.

Row 2: Knit.

Bind off as to purl.

Pretty Pink Tunic (for child)

■■■□ INTERMEDIATE

Sizes:
2   4   6   8   10   12

Finished Chest Size:
27"   28½"   30"   32"   34"   36"

Note: Instructions are written for Size 2; changes for other sizes are in parentheses.

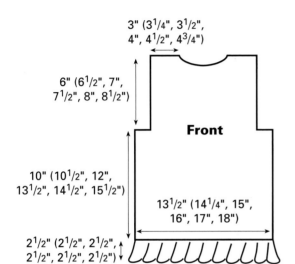

3" (3¹/4", 3¹/2", 4", 4¹/2", 4³/4")

6" (6¹/2", 7", 7¹/2", 8", 8¹/2")

Front

10" (10¹/2", 12", 13¹/2", 14¹/2", 15¹/2")

13¹/2" (14¹/4", 15", 16", 17", 18")

2¹/2" (2¹/2", 2¹/2", 2¹/2", 2¹/2", 2¹/2")

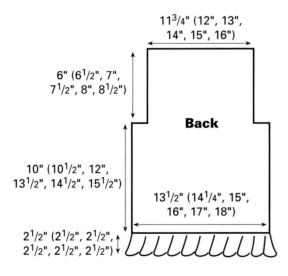

11³/4" (12", 13", 14", 15", 16")

6" (6¹/2", 7", 7¹/2", 8", 8¹/2")

Back

10" (10¹/2", 12", 13¹/2", 14¹/2", 15¹/2")

13¹/2" (14¹/4", 15", 16", 17", 18")

2¹/2" (2¹/2", 2¹/2", 2¹/2", 2¹/2", 2¹/2")

These measurements for child's sweater sizes are approximate.

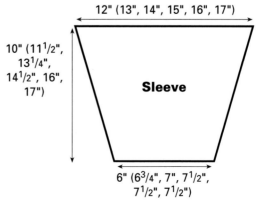

12" (13", 14", 15", 16", 17")

10" (11¹/2", 13¹/4", 14¹/2", 16", 17")

Sleeve

6" (6³/4", 7", 7¹/2", 7¹/2", 7¹/2")

Materials:
Fine (sport weight) yarn, 10 (10, 12½, 12½, 15, 17½) oz [672 (672, 840, 840, 1008, 1176) yds, 280 (280, 350, 350, 420, 490) gms] pink
Note: Our photographed sweater was made with Lion Brand Micro Spun, Peppermint Pink #101.
Size 8 (5mm) straight knitting needles, or size required for gauge
Size 5 (3.75mm) straight knitting needles
Size 5 (3.75mm) 16" circular knitting needle (for neck)
Size 18 tapestry needle

Gauge:
With larger size needles in stockinette stitch (knit one row, purl one row):
5 sts = 1"

Special Abbreviations

Slip, Slip, Knit (SSK):
Slip next 2 sts one at a time from the left needle to the right needle, insert the left needle into the fronts of these two stitches and knit them together—SSK made.

Make 1 (M1):
Insert left needle from front to back under horizontal strand between the last stitch worked and the next stitch on the left needle; knit this strand through the back loop—M1 made.

Instructions

Back
With larger size needles, cast on 163 (173, 183, 193, 213, 223) sts.

Ruffle Border:
Row 1 (wrong side): K3; * P7, K3; rep from * 15 (16, 17, 18, 20, 21) times more.

Row 2 (right side): P3; * K7, P3; rep from * 15 (16, 17, 18, 20, 21) times more.

Row 3: Rep Row 1.

Row 4: P3; * K2, sl next 2 sts as to knit, K1, P2SSO; K2, P3; rep from * 15 (16, 17, 18, 20, 21) times more—131 (139, 147, 155, 171, 179) sts.

Row 5: K3; * P5, K3; rep from * across.

Row 6: P3; * K5, P3; rep from * across.

Row 7: Rep Row 5.

Row 8: P3; * K1, sl next 2 sts as to knit, K1, P2SSO; K1, P3; rep from * across—99 (105, 111, 117, 129, 135) sts.

Row 9: K3; * P3, K3; rep from * across.

Row 10: P3; * K3, P3; rep from * across.

Row 11: Rep Row 9.

Row 12: P3; * sl next 2 sts as to knit, K1, P2SSO; P3—67 (71, 75, 79, 87, 91) sts.

Row 13: K3; * P1, K3; rep from * across.

Row 14: P3; * K1, P3; rep from * across.

Row 15: K3: * P1, K3; rep from * across.

Row 16: Rep Row 14.

Body:
Row 1 (wrong side): Purl.

Row 2 (right side): Knit.

Rows 3, 5, 7, 9, 11, 13 and 15: Purl.

Row 4: K5 (7, 5, 7, 7, 5); * K2 tog; YO; K6; rep from * 6 (6, 7, 7, 8, 9) times more; K2 tog; YO; K4 (6, 4, 6, 6, 4).

Row 6: K3 (5, 3, 5, 5, 3); * K2 tog, YO; K1, YO; SSK (see Special Abbreviations); K3; rep from * 6 (6, 7, 7, 8, 9) times more; K2 tog; YO; K1, YO; SSK; K3 (5, 3, 5, 5, 3).

Row 8: Rep Row 4.

Row 10: Knit.

Row 12: K9 (11, 9, 11, 11, 9); * K2 tog; YO; K6; rep from * 5 (5, 6, 6, 7, 8) times more; K2 tog; YO; K8 (10, 8, 10, 10, 8).

Row 14: K8 (10, 8, 10, 10, 8); * K2 tog; YO; K1, YO; SSK; K3; rep from * 5 (5, 6, 6, 7, 8) times more; K2 tog; YO; K1, YO; SSK, K6 (8, 6, 8, 8, 6).

Row 16: Rep Row 14.

Rep Rows 1 through 16 until piece measures about 12½" (13", 14½", 16", 17", 18") from cast-on edge, ending by working a wrong side row.

Armhole Shaping:
Row 1 (right side): Bind off 4 (5, 5, 5, 5, 5) sts; work in pattern across.

Row 2: Bind off 4 (5, 5, 5, 5, 5) sts; purl across—59 (61, 65, 69, 77, 81) sts.

Continue in pattern as established until piece measures about 18½" (19½", 21½", 23½", 25", 26½") from cast-on edge.

Bind off.

Front
Work same as Back to Armhole Shaping.

Armhole Shaping:
Row 1 (right side): Bind off 4 (5, 5, 5, 5, 5) sts; work in pattern across.

Row 2: Bind off 4 (5, 5, 5, 5, 5) sts; purl across—59 (61, 65, 69, 77, 81) sts.

Continue in pattern as established until piece measures 16" (16¾", 18½", 20½", 22", 23½") from cast-on edge, ending by working a right side row.

Neck Shaping:

Row 1 (wrong side): For right shoulder, P23 (24, 25, 27, 31, 33) sts; join second skein of yarn, for neck, bind off next 13 (13, 15, 15, 15, 15) sts; for left shoulder, purl rem sts—23 (24, 25, 27, 31, 33) sts on each shoulder.

Note: Work both shoulders at same time with separate skeins of yarn.

Row 2 (right side): For left shoulder, work in pattern to last 4 sts; K2 tog; K2; for right shoulder, K2, SSK; work in pattern across—22 (23, 24, 26, 30, 32) sts on each shoulder.

Row 3: Purl across both shoulders.

Rows 4 through 15 (15, 15, 15, 17, 19): Rep Rows 2 and 3 six (6, 6, 6, 7, 8) times more. At end of last row—16 (17, 18, 20, 23, 24) sts on each shoulder.

Continue to work in pattern as established until piece measures 18½" (19½", 21½", 23½", 25", 26½") from cast-on edge.

Bind off.

Sleeve (make 2)

With smaller size straight needles, cast on 32 (34, 36, 38, 38, 38) sts.

Border:

Row 1: Knit.

Rows 2 through 4: Rep Row 1.

Row 5: K6 (6, 6, 7, 7, 7), M1(see Special Abbreviations); * K10 (11, 12, 12, 12, 12), M1; rep from * once more; K6 (6, 6, 7, 7, 7)—35 (37, 39, 41, 41, 41) sts.

Change to larger size needles.

Body:

Row 1 (wrong side): Purl.

Row 2 (right side): K2, M1; knit to last 2 sts; M1, K2—37 (39, 41, 43, 43, 43) sts.

Rows 3, 5, 7, 9, 11, 13 and 15: Purl.

Row 4: K2 (3, 4, 5, 5, 5); * K2 tog; YO; K6; rep from * 3 times more; K2 tog; YO; K1 (2, 3, 4, 4, 4).

For Size 2 Only:

Row 6: K1; * K2 tog; YO; K1, YO; SSK; K3; rep from * 3 times more; K2 tog; YO; K2.

Continue with For All Sizes below.

For Sizes 4, 6, 8, 10 and 12 Only:

Row 6: K2 (3, 4, 4, 4); * K2 tog; YO; K1, YO; SSK; K3; rep from * 3 times more; K2 tog; YO; K1, YO; SSK; K0 (1, 2, 2, 2).

Continue with For All Sizes.

For All Sizes:

Row 8: K1, M1; K1 (2, 3, 4, 4, 4); * K2 tog; YO; K6; rep from * 3 times more; K2 tog; YO; M1, K1 (2, 3, 4, 4, 4)—39 (41, 43, 45, 45, 45) sts.

Row 10: Knit.

Row 12: K1, M1; K5 (6, 7, 8, 8, 8); * K2 tog; YO; K6; rep from * 3 times more; K0 (1, 2, 3, 3, 3), M1; K1—41 (43, 45, 47, 47, 47) sts.

Row 14: K6 (7, 8, 9, 9, 9); * K2 tog; YO; K1, YO; SSK; K3; rep from * 3 times more; K3 (4, 5, 6, 6, 6).

Row 16: K1, M1; K6 (7, 8, 9, 9, 9); * K2 tog; YO; K6; rep from * 3 times more; K1 (2, 3, 4, 4, 4), M1; K1—43 (45, 47, 49, 49, 49) sts.

Continue in pattern inc one st each end every 4th row 8 (10, 11, 13, 15, 19) times more—59 (65, 69, 75, 79, 87) sts.

Continue even (without inc) in pattern until piece measures about 10" (11½", 13¼", 14½", 16", 17") from cast-on edge.

Bind off.

Assembly

Sew shoulder seams. Sew sleeves to front and back beginning and ending above bound off armhole stitches and having center of bound off edge of sleeve at shoulder seam. Sew sleeve and side seams.

Neck Edging

Hold tunic with right sides facing you and neck edge at top; with circular needle pick up 76 (80, 88, 88, 88, 90) sts evenly spaced around neck edge.

Row 1: Purl.

Row 2: Knit.

Row 3: Purl.

Row 4: Knit.

Bind off as to purl.

True Blue Mock Cable

True Blue Mock Cable (for doll)

⬛⬛⬛◻ INTERMEDIATE

Size:
18" doll

Finished Chest Size:
14"

Materials:
Light (worsted weight) yarn, 5 oz (236 yds, 142 gms) blue
Note: *Our photographed sweater was made with Lion Brand Cotton Ease, Candy Blue #107.*
Size 8 (5mm) straight knitting needles, or size required for gauge
Size 5 (3.75mm) straight knitting needles
Size 5 (3.75mm) double-pointed knitting needles (for neck)
Size 18 tapestry needle

Gauge:
With larger size needles in stockinette stitch (knit one row, purl one row):
21 sts = 4"

Special Abbreviations

Make 1 (M1):
Insert left needle from front to back under horizontal strand between the last stitch worked and the next stitch on the left needle; knit this strand through the back loop—M1 made.

Slip, Slip, Knit (SSK):
Slip next 2 sts one at a time from the left needle to the right needle, insert the left needle into the front of these two stitches and knit them together—SSK made.

Pattern Stitch

Mock Cable (mock cable):
Slip 1 as to purl, K2, YO, pass slipped st over K2 and YO—mock cable made.

Instructions

Back

With smaller size straight needles, cast on 36 sts.

Ribbing:
Row 1 (right side): * K1, P1; rep from * across.

Rows 2 through 5: Rep Row 1.

Row 6: (K1, P1) 3 times; M1 (see Special Abbreviations); * (K1, P1) 6 times; M1; rep from * once more; (K1, P1) 3 times—39 sts.

Change to larger size needles.

Body:

Row 1 (right side): K1, P3; * K3, P4; rep from * 3 times more; K3, P3, K1.

Row 2: P1, K3; * P3, K4; rep from * 3 times more; P3, K3 P1.

Row 3: K1, P3; * mock cable (see Pattern Stitch) over next 3 sts; P4; rep from * 3 times more; mock cable over next 3 sts; P3, K1.

Row 4: Rep Row 2.

Rep Rows 1 through 4 until piece measures about 3" from cast-on edge, ending by working a wrong side row.

Armhole Shaping:

Continue in pattern as established.

Row 1 (right side): Bind off 1 st; work in pattern across—38 sts.

Row 2: Bind off 1 st; work in pattern across—37 sts.

Work even in pattern until piece measures about 6" from cast-on edge, ending by working a wrong side row.

Bind off.

Front

Work same as Back until piece measures about 4½" from cast-on edge, ending by working a wrong side row.

Neck Shaping:

Row 1 (right side): For left shoulder, work in pattern across first 14 sts; join second skein of yarn, for neck, bind off 9 sts; for right shoulder, work in pattern across—14 sts on each shoulder.

Note: *Work both shoulders at same time with separate skeins of yarn.*

Row 2: For right shoulder, work in pattern to last 3 sts; K2 tog; K1; for left shoulder, K1, SSK (see Special Abbreviations); work in pattern across—13 sts on each shoulder.

Row 3: Work in pattern across both shoulders.

Rows 4 through 9: Rep Rows 2 and 3 three times more. At end of Row 9—10 sts on each shoulder.

Work even in pattern until piece measures about 6" from cast-on edge, ending by working a wrong side row.

Bind off.

Sew shoulder seams.

Sleeve

Hold piece with right side facing you and one armhole edge at top; with smaller size straight needles, pick up 33 sts evenly spaced along armhole edge, beginning and ending above bound off sts of armhole shaping and having same number of sts on front and back and one at shoulder seam.

Change to larger size needles.

Row 1 (wrong side): P1, K7, (P3, K4) twice; P3, K7, P1.

Row 2 (right side): K1, P7, (mock cable over next 3 sts, P4) twice; mock cable over next 3 sts; P7, K1—3 cables.

Row 3: Rep Row 1.

Row 4: K1, P7, (K3, P4) twice; K3, P7, K1.

Row 5: P1, SSK; K5, (P3, K4) twice; P3, K5, K2 tog; P1—31 sts.

Row 6: K1, P6, (mock cable, P4) twice; mock cable, P6, K1.

Row 7: P1, K6, (P3, K4) twice; P3, K6, P1.

Row 8: Rep Row 6.

Row 9: P1, SSK; K4, (P3, K4) twice; P3, K4, K2 tog; P1—29 sts.

Rows 10 through 21: Continue in pattern decreasing one st each end every 4th row 3 times more, working partial pattern repeats in reverse stockinette stitch (purl one row, knit one row). At end of Row 21—23 sts.

Row 22 (right side): K1, P2, (mock cable, P4) twice; mock cable; P2, K1.

Row 23: P1, K2, P3, K4, P1, P2 tog; K4, P3, K2, P1—22 sts.

Change to smaller size needles.

Ribbing:

Row 1 (right side): K1, P1; rep from * across.

Rows 2 through 6: Rep Row 1.

Bind off loosely in ribbing.

Rep for other sleeve.

Assembly

Sew side edges at top of sleeve to bound off sts of front and back armholes. Sew sleeve and side seams.

Neck Edging

Hold piece with right side facing you and neck edge at top; beginning at one shoulder seam, with double-pointed needles pick up 42 sts evenly spaced around neck edge.

Rnd 1: * K1, P1; rep from * around.

Rnds 2 through 5: Rep Rnd 1.

Bind off loosely in ribbing.

True Blue Mock Cable (for child)

◼◼◼◻ ▭ INTERMEDIATE

Sizes:
2   4   6   8   10   12

Finished Chest Size:
27"   28½"   30"   32"   34"   36"

Note: Instructions are written for Size 2; changes for other sizes are in parentheses.

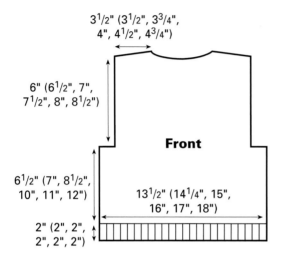

3½" (3½", 3¾", 4", 4½", 4¾")

6" (6½", 7", 7½", 8", 8½")

Front

6½" (7", 8½", 10", 11", 12")

13½" (14¼", 15", 16", 17", 18")

2" (2", 2", 2", 2", 2")

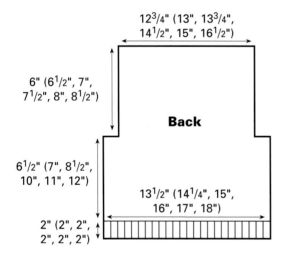

12¾" (13", 13¾", 14½", 15", 16½")

6" (6½", 7", 7½", 8", 8½")

Back

6½" (7", 8½", 10", 11", 12")

13½" (14¼", 15", 16", 17", 18")

2" (2", 2", 2", 2", 2")

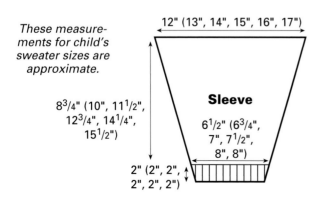

These measurements for child's sweater sizes are approximate.

12" (13", 14", 15", 16", 17")

Sleeve

8¾" (10", 11½", 12¾", 14¼", 15½")

6½" (6¾", 7", 7½", 8", 8")

2" (2", 2", 2", 2", 2")

Materials:
Fine (sport weight) yarn, 11 (11, 14, 14, 18, 18) oz [300 (300, 400, 400, 500, 500) yds, 621 (621, 828, 828, 1035, 1035) gms] blue
Note: Our photographed sweater was made with Lion Brand Cotton Ease, Candy Blue #107.
Size 8 (5mm) straight knitting needles, or size required for gauge
Size 5 (3.75mm) straight knitting needle
Size 5 (3.75mm) 16" circular knitting needle (for neck)
Size 18 tapestry needle

Gauge:
With larger size needles in stockinette stitch (knit one row, purl one row):
21 sts = 4"

Special Abbreviations

Make 1 (M1):
Insert left needle from front to back under horizontal strand between the last stitch worked and the next stitch on the left needle; knit this strand through the back loop—M1 made.

Slip, Slip, Knit (SSK):
Slip next 2 sts one at a time from the left needle to the right needle, insert the left needle into the fronts of these two stitches and knit them together—SSK made.

Pattern Stitch

Mock Cable (mock cable):
Slip 1 as to purl, K2, YO, pass slipped st over K2 and YO—mock cable made.

Instructions

Back
With smaller size straight needles, cast on 66 (70, 72, 76, 80, 86) sts.

Ribbing:
Row 1 (right side): * K1, P1; rep from * across.

Rows 2 through 13: Rep Row 1.

Row 14: Continuing in pattern as established, work 6 (5, 6, 7, 5, 7) sts, M1 (see Special Abbreviations); * work 11 (10, 8, 9, 10, 9) sts, M1; rep from * 4 (5, 7, 6, 6, 7) times more; work 5 (5, 4, 6, 5, 7) sts—72 (77, 81, 84, 88, 95) sts.

Change to larger size needles.

Body:
Row 1 (right side): P3 (2, 4, 2, 4, 4), K3; * P4, K3; rep from * 8 (9, 9, 10, 10, 11) times more; P3 (2, 4, 2, 4, 4).

Row 2: K3 (2, 4, 2, 4, 4), P3; * K4, P3; rep from * 8 (9, 9, 10, 10, 11) times more; K3 (2, 4, 2, 4, 4).

Row 3: P3 (2, 4, 2, 4, 4), mock cable (see Pattern Stitch) over next 3 sts; * P4, mock cable over next 3 sts; rep from * 8 (9, 9, 10, 10, 11) times more; P3 (2, 4, 2, 4, 4).

Row 4: Rep Row 2.

Rep Rows 1 through 4 until piece measures about 8½" (9",10½", 12", 13", 14") from cast-on edge, ending by working a wrong side row.

Armhole Shaping:
Row 1 (right side): Bind off 4 (6, 6, 6, 6, 6) sts; work in pattern across.

Row 2: Bind off 4 (6, 6, 6, 6, 6) sts; work in pattern across—64 (65, 69, 72, 76, 83) sts.

Work in pattern as established until armhole measures about 6" (6½", 7", 7½", 8", 8½"), ending by working a wrong side row.

Bind off.

Front
Work same as Back until armhole measures about 3½" (3¾", 4", 4½", 5", 5½") from cast-on edge, ending by working a wrong side row.

Neck Shaping:
Row 1 (right side): For left shoulder, work in pattern across first 24 (24, 26, 28, 30, 32) sts; join second skein of yarn, for neck, bind off 16 (17, 17, 16, 16, 19) sts; for right shoulder, work in pattern across.

Note: Work both shoulders at the same time with separate skeins of yarn.

Row 2: For right shoulder, work in pattern to last 4 sts; K2 tog; P2; for left shoulder, P2, SSK (see Special Abbreviations); work in pattern across—23 (23, 25, 27, 29, 31) sts on each shoulder.

Row 3: For left shoulder, work in pattern to last 3 sts; P1, K2; for right shoulder, K2, P1, work in pattern across.

Rows 4 through 15 (15, 17, 17, 15, 17): Rep Rows 2 and 3 six (6, 7, 7, 6, 7) times more. At end of last row—17 (17, 18, 20, 23, 24) sts on each shoulder.

Work even in pattern until armhole measures about 6" (6½", 7", 7½", 8", 8½"), ending by working a wrong side row.

Bind off.

Sew shoulder seams.

Sleeve
Hold piece with right side facing you and one armhole edge at top, with smaller size straight needles, pick up 63 (67, 74, 81, 84, 90) sts along armhole edge beginning and ending above bound off sts of armhole shaping and having the same number of sts on front and back.

Change to larger size needles.

Row 1 (wrong side): K9 (11, 11, 11, 9, 12), P3; * K4, P3; rep from * 5 (5, 6, 7, 8, 8) times more; K9 (11, 11, 11, 9, 12).

Row 2 (right side): P9 (11, 11, 11, 9, 12), K3; * P4, K3; rep from * 5 (5, 6, 7, 8, 8) times more; K9 (11, 11, 11, 9, 12).

Row 3: K2, SSK; K5 (7, 7, 7, 5, 8), P3; * K4, P3; rep from * 5 (5, 6, 7, 8, 8) times more; K5 (7, 7, 7, 5, 8), K2 tog; K2—61 (65, 72, 79, 82, 88) sts.

Row 4: P8 (10, 10, 10, 8, 11), mock cable over next 3 sts; * P4, mock cable over next 3 sts; rep from * 5 (5, 6, 7, 8, 8) times more; P8 (10, 10, 10, 8, 11)—7 (7, 8, 9, 10, 10) cables.

Row 5: K8 (10, 10, 10, 8, 11), P3; * K4, P3; rep from * 5 (5, 6, 7, 8, 8) times more; K8 (10, 10, 10, 8, 11).

Row 6: P8 (10, 10, 10, 8, 11), K3; * P4, K3; rep from * 5 (5, 6, 7, 8, 8) times more; P8 (10, 10, 10, 8, 11).

Row 7: K2, SSK; K4 (6, 6, 6, 4, 7), P3; * K4, P3; rep from * 5 (5, 6, 7, 8, 8) times more; K4 (6, 6, 6, 4, 7)—59 (63, 70, 77, 80, 86) sts.

Row 8: P7 (9, 9, 9, 7, 10), mock cable; * P4, mock cable; rep from * 5 (5, 6, 7, 8, 8) times more; P7 (9, 9, 9, 7, 10).

Row 9: K7 (9, 9, 9, 7, 10), P3; * K4, P3; rep from * 5 (5, 6, 7, 8, 8) times more; K7 (9, 9, 9, 7, 10).

Row 10: Rep Row 8.

Row 11: K2, SSK; K3 (5, 5, 5, 3, 6), P3; * K4, P3; rep from * 5 (5, 6, 7, 8, 8) times more; K3 (5, 5, 5, 3, 6), K2 tog; K2—57 (59, 66, 73, 76, 82) sts.

Continue in pattern dec one st each end every 4th row 10 (11, 13, 16, 16, 19) times more, working partial pattern repeats at each end in reverse stockinette st (purl one row, knit one row). At end of last decrease row—37 (39, 42, 43, 46, 46) sts.

Continue in pattern working even (without dec) until sleeve measures about 8¾" (10", 11½", 12¾", 14¼", 15½"), ending by working a right side row.

Next Row: Continuing in pattern, work 6 (6, 5, 7, 6, 6) sts, K2 tog; * work 10 (11, 8, 12, 9, 9) sts, K2 tog; rep from * once (once, twice, once, twice, twice) more; work 5 (5, 5, 6, 5, 5) sts—34 (36, 38, 40, 42, 42) sts.

Change to smaller size needles.

Ribbing:
Row 1 (right side): K1, P1; rep from * across.

Rows 2 through 13: Rep Row 1.

Bind off loosely in ribbing.

Rep for other sleeve.

Assembly
Sew side edges at top of sleeve to bound off sts of front and back armholes. Sew sleeve and side seams.

Neck Edging
Hold piece with right side facing you and neck edge at top; beginning at one shoulder seam, with circular needle pick up 76 (86, 86, 86, 90) sts evenly spaced around neck edge.

Rnd 1: * K1, P1; rep from * around.

Rnds 2 through 5: Rep Rnd 1.

Bind off loosely in ribbing.

Super Stripe Raglan

Super Stripe Raglan (for doll)

◼◼◼◼▢ INTERMEDIATE

Size:
18" doll

Finished Chest Size:
14"

Materials:
Fine (sport weight) yarn, 2½ oz (168 yds, 70 gms) each black, white and red
Note: *Our photographed sweater was made with Lion Brand Micro Spun, Ebony #153, Lily white #100 and Cherry Red #113*
Size 8 (5mm) straight knitting needles, or size required for gauge
Size 5 (3.75mm) straight knitting needles
Size 5 (3.75mm) double-pointed needles (for neck)
Size 18 tapestry needle

Gauge:
With larger size needles in stockinette stitch (knit one row, purl one row):
5 sts = 1"

Special Abbreviations

Make 1 (M1):
Insert left needle from front to back under horizontal strand between the last stitch worked and the next stitch on the left needle; knit this strand through the back loop—M1 made.

Slip, Slip, Knit (SSK):
Slip next 2 sts one at a time from the left needle to the right needle, insert the left needle into the fronts of these two stitches and knit them together—SSK made.

Instructions

Back
With smaller size straight needles and black, cast on 40 sts.

Ribbing:
Row 1: * K1, P1; rep from * across.

Rows 2 through 7: Rep Row 1.

Row 8: K1, (P1, K1) twice; M1 (see Special Abbreviations); * (P1, K1) 5 times, M1; rep from * twice more; (P1, K1) twice; P1—44 sts.

Change to larger size needles.

Body:
Row 1 (right side): Knit.

Row 2: Purl.

Rep Rows 1 and 2 in the following color sequence:

5 rows black

3 rows white

5 rows black

3 rows white

5 rows black

3 rows white

4 rows black

Armhole Shaping:

Row 1 (right side): With black, bind off 3 sts; knit across.

Row 2: Bind off 3 sts; purl across—38 sts.

Row 3: K2, SSK (see Special Abbreviations on page 31); knit to last 4 sts; K2 tog; K2—36 sts.

Row 4: Purl.

Row 5: With red, K2, SSK; knit to last 4 sts; K2 tog; K2—34 sts.

Row 6: Purl.

Rows 7 and 8: Rep Rows 5 and 6. At end of Row 8—32 sts.

Row 9: Rep Row 5—30 sts

Row 10: With black, purl.

Rows 11 through 22: With black, rep Rows 5 and 6 six times more—18 sts.

Bind off.

Front

Work same as Back through Row 10 of Armhole Shaping.

Armhole Shaping:

Rows 11 and 12: With black, rep Rows 5 and 6. At end of Row 12—28 sts.

Neck Shaping:

Row 1 (right side): For left shoulder, K2, SSK; K6; join second skein of yarn, for neck, bind off 8; for right shoulder, knit to last 4 sts, K2 tog; K2—9 sts on each shoulder.

Note: *Work both shoulders at same time with separate skeins of yarn.*

Row 2: Purl across both shoulders.

Row 3: For left shoulder, K2, SSK; K3, K2 tog; for right shoulder, SSK; K3, K2 tog; K2—7 sts on each shoulder.

Row 4: Purl.

Row 5: For left shoulder, K2, SSK; K1, K2 tog; for right shoulder, SSK, K1, K2 tog; K2—5 sts on each shoulder.

Row 6: Purl.

Row 7: For left shoulder, K1, SSK; K2 tog; for right shoulder, SSK, K2 tog; K1—3 sts on each shoulder.

Row 8: Purl.

Bind off.

Sleeve (make 2)

With smaller size straight needles and black, cast on 24 sts.

Ribbing:

Row 1: * K1 P1; rep from * across.

Rows 2 through 7: Rep row 1.

Row 8: (K1, P1) 3 times, M1; (K1, P1) 6 times, M1; (K1, P1) 3 times—26 sts.

Change to larger size needles.

Body:

Row 1 (right side): Knit.

Row 2: Purl.

Row 3: K2, M1; knit to last 2 sts; M1, K2—28 sts.

Row 4: Purl.

Rows 5 through 12: Rep Rows 1 and 2.

Row 13: With white, knit.

Row 14: Purl.

Row 15: Knit.

Row 16: With black, purl.

Row 17: Knit.

Row 18: P2, M1; purl to last 2 sts; M1; P2—30 sts.

Rep Rows 1 and 2 in following color sequence:

2 rows black

3 rows white

5 rows black

3 rows white

2 rows black

Sleeve Cap Shaping:

Row 1 (right side): With black, bind off 3 sts; knit across.

Row 2: Bind off 3 sts; purl across—24 sts.

Row 3: K2, SSK; knit to last 4 sts; K2 tog; K2—22 sts.

Row 4: Purl.

Rows 5 and 6: Rep Rows 3 and 4. At end of Row 6—20 sts.

Row 7: With red, K2, SSK; knit to last 4 sts, K2 tog; K2—18 sts.

Row 8: Purl.

Rows 9 and 10: With red, rep Rows 7 and 8—16 sts.

Row 11: Rep Row 7—14 sts.

Row 12: With black, purl.

Rows 13 through 22: With black, rep Rows 7 and 8—4 sts. Bind off.

Assembly

Sew sleeves to front and back. Sew sleeve and side seams.

Neck Ribbing

With double-pointed needles and black, pick up 46 sts evenly spaced around neck.

Rnd 1 (right side): * K1, P1; rep from * around.

Rnds 2 through 5: Rep Rnd 1.

Bind off loosely in ribbing.

Super Stripe Raglan (for child)

◖◖◖◻ INTERMEDIATE

Sizes:
2   4   6   8   10   12

Finished Chest Size:
27"   28½"   30"   32"   34"   36"

Note: Instructions are written for Size 2; changes for other sizes are in parentheses.

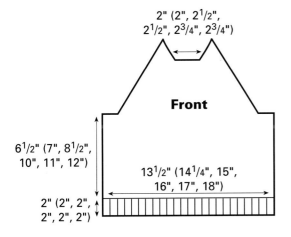

2" (2", 2½", 2½", 2³/₄", 2³/₄")

Front

6¹/₂" (7", 8¹/₂", 10", 11", 12")

13¹/₂" (14¹/₄", 15", 16", 17", 18")

2" (2", 2", 2", 2", 2")

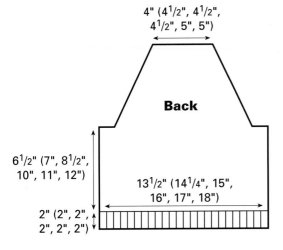

4" (4¹/₂", 4¹/₂", 4¹/₂", 5", 5")

Back

6¹/₂" (7", 8¹/₂", 10", 11", 12")

13¹/₂" (14¹/₄", 15", 16", 17", 18")

2" (2", 2", 2", 2", 2")

These measurements for child's sweater sizes are approximate.

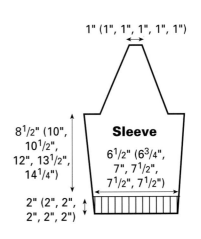

1" (1", 1", 1", 1", 1")

Sleeve

8¹/₂" (10", 10¹/₂", 12", 13¹/₂", 14¹/₄")

6¹/₂" (6³/₄", 7", 7¹/₂", 7¹/₂", 7¹/₂")

2" (2", 2", 2", 2", 2")

Materials:

Fine (sport weight) yarn, 7½ (7½, 10, 10, 12½, 15) oz [504 (504, 672, 672, 840) yds, 210 (210, 280, 280, 350, 420) gms] black; 2½ oz (168 yds, 70 gms] each, white and red

Note: *Our photographed sweater was made with Lion Brand Micro Spun, Ebony #153, Lily white #100 and Cherry Red #113.*

Size 8 (5mm) straight knitting needles, or size required for gauge

Size 5 (3.75mm) straight knitting needles

Size 5 (3.75mm) 16" circular knitting needle (for neck)

Size 18 tapestry needle

Gauge:

With larger size needles in stockinette stitch (knit one row, purl one row):

5 sts = 1"

6 rows = 1"

Special Abbreviations

Make 1 (M1):

Insert left needle from front to back under horizontal strand between the last stitch worked and the next stitch on the left needle; knit this strand through the back loop—M1 made.

Slip, Slip, Knit (SSK):

Slip next 2 sts one at a time from the left needle to the right needle, insert the left needle into the fronts of these two stitches and knit them together—SSK made.

Instructions

Back

With smaller size straight needles and black, cast on 62 (66, 68, 72, 78, 82) sts.

Ribbing:

Row 1: * K1, P1; rep from * across.

Rows 2 through 15: Rep Row 1.

Row 12: Continuing in pattern as established, work 6 (6, 6, 4, 8, 6) sts, M1 (see Special Abbreviations); * work 10 (11, 8, 9, 9, 10) sts, M1; rep from * 4 (4, 6, 6, 6,6) times more; work 6 (5, 6, 5, 7, 6) sts—68 (72, 76, 80, 86, 90) sts.

Change to larger size needles.

Body:

Row 1 (right side): Knit.

Row 2: Purl.

Rep Rows 1 and 2 until piece measures about 3½" (3½", 5", 6½", 7½", 8½") from cast-on edge, ending by working a wrong side row.

Rep Rows 1 and 2 in the following color sequence:

5 rows white

8 rows black

5 rows white

8 rows black

5 rows white

7 rows black

Armhole Shaping:

Row 1 (right side): With black, bind off 6 (6, 6, 6, 7, 8) sts; knit across.

Row 2: Bind off 6 (6, 6, 6, 7, 8) sts; purl across—56 (60, 64, 68, 72, 74) sts.

Row 3: K2, SSK (see Special Abbreviations); knit to last 4 sts; K2 tog; K2—54 (58, 62, 66, 70, 72) sts.

Row 4: Purl.

Row 5: K2, SSK; knit to last 4 sts; K2 tog; K2.

Row 6: Purl.

Rows 7 through 14: With red, rep Rows 5 and 6 four times more. At end of Row 14—46 (50, 54, 58, 62, 64) sts.

Rows 15 through 40 (42, 46, 50, 50, 52): With black, rep Rows 5 and 6 thirteen (14, 16, 18, 18, 19) times. At end of last row—20 (22, 22, 22, 26, 26) sts.

Row 41 (43, 47, 51, 51, 53): Knit.

Row 42 (46, 48, 54, 56, 60): Purl.

Bind off.

Front

Work same as Back to Armhole Shaping.

Armhole Shaping:

Row 1 (right side): Bind off 6 (6, 6, 6, 7, 8) sts; knit across.

Row 2: Bind off 6 (6, 6, 6, 7, 8) sts; purl across—56 (60, 64, 68, 72, 74) sts.

Row 3: K2, SSK (see Special Abbreviations); knit to last 4 sts; K2 tog; K2—54 (58, 62, 66, 70, 72) sts.

Row 4: Purl.

Row 5: K2, SSK; knit to last 4 sts; K2 tog; K2.

Row 6: Purl.

Rows 7 through 14: With red, rep Rows 5 and 6 three times. At end of Row 14—46 (50, 54, 58, 62, 64) sts.

Rows 15 through 22 (22, 24, 26, 30, 30): With black, rep Rows 5 and 6 four (4, 5, 6, 9, 9) times more. At end of last row—38 (42, 44, 46, 46, 48) sts.

Neck Shaping:
Row 1 (right side): For left shoulder, K2, SSK; K10 (12; 12, 13, 12, 13); join second skein of yarn, for neck, bind off 10 (10, 12, 12, 14, 14); for right shoulder, knit to last 4 sts, K2 tog; K2—13 (15, 15, 16, 15, 16) sts on each shoulder.

Note: Work both shoulders at same time with separate skeins of yarn.

Row 2: Purl across each shoulder.

Row 3: For left shoulder, K2, SSK; knit to last 4 sts; K2 tog; K2; for right shoulder, K2, SSK; work to last 4 sts; K2 tog; K2—11 (13, 13, 14, 13, 14) sts on each shoulder

Row 4: Purl.

Rows 5 through 12 (12, 12, 12, 14, 14): Rep Rows 3 and 4 four (4, 4, 4, 5, 5) times more. At end of last row—3 (5, 5, 6, 3, 4) sts.

Row 13 (13, 13, 13, 15, 15): For left shoulder, K2, SSK; knit across; for right shoulder, knit to last 4 sts; K2 tog; K2—2 (4, 4, 5, 2, 3) sts.

Row 14 (14, 14, 14, 16, 16): Purl.

Rep last two rows until 1 st remains.

Finish off.

Sleeve (make 2)
With smaller size needles and black, cast on 32 (34, 36, 38, 38, 38) sts.

Ribbing:
Row 1: * K1 P1; rep from * across.

Rows 2 through 15: Rep Row 1.

Row 16: Continuing in pattern as established, work 4 (5, 5, 6, 6, 6) sts, M1; * work 8 (8, 9, 9, 9, 9) sts, M1; rep from * twice more; work 4 (5, 4, 5, 5, 5) sts—36 (38, 40, 42, 42, 42) sts.

Change to larger size needles.

Body:
Row 1 (right side): Knit.

Row 2: Purl.

Rows 3 through 6: Rep Rows 1 and 2 twice.

Row 7: K2, M1; knit to last 2 sts; M1; K2—38 (40, 42, 44, 44, 44) sts.

Row 8: Purl.

Continue working in stockinette stitch (knit one row, purl one row) inc one st each end every 6th (7th, 7th, 7th, 7th, 7th) rows 8 (8, 9, 10, 11, 13) times more—54 (56, 60, 64, 66, 70) sts while working in the following color sequence:

Note: When increases have been completed work even (without increases) in stockinette st.

24 (34, 38, 50, 60, 64) rows black

5 rows white

8 rows black

5 rows white

7 rows black

5 rows white

7 rows black.

Sleeve Cap Shaping:
Row 1 (right side): With black, bind off 6 (6, 6, 6, 7, 8) sts; knit across.

Row 2: Bind off 6 (6, 6, 6, 7, 8) sts; purl across—42 (44, 48, 52, 52, 54) sts.

Row 3: K2, SSK; knit to last 4 sts; K2 tog; K2—40 (42, 46, 50, 50, 52) sts.

Row 4: Purl.

Rows 5 and 6: Rep Rows 3 and 4—38 (40, 44, 48, 48, 50) sts.

Rows 7 through 14: With red, rep Rows 3 and 4 four times—30 (32, 36, 40, 40, 42) sts.

Rows 15 and 16: With black, rep Rows 3 and 4—28 (30, 34, 38, 38, 40) sts.

Continuing in stockinette st with black, dec at each end of every other row 5 (6, 9, 12, 8, 7) times more; then dec at beg and end of every 3rd row 6 (6, 5, 4, 8, 10) times. At end of last dec row—6 sts.

Bind off.

Assembly
Sew sleeves to front and back matching stripes. Sew sleeve and side seams.

Neck Ribbing
With smaller size circular needle and black, pick up 80 (84, 92, 92, 94, 94) sts evenly spaced around neck.

Rnd 1 (right side): * K1, P1; rep from * around.

Rnds 2 through 7: Rep Rnd 1.

Bind off loosely in ribbing.

Cool Blue Gansey

Cool Blue Gansey (for doll)

■■■□ INTERMEDIATE

Size:
18" Doll

Finished Chest Size:
14"

Materials
Light (worsted weight) yarn, 5 oz (236 yds, 142 gms) blue

Note: *Our photographed sweater was made with Lion Brand Cotton Ease, Ice Blue #106.*

Size 8 (5mm) knitting needles, or size required for gauge
Size 5 (3.75mm) straight knitting needle
Size 5 (3.75mm) double-pointed needles (for doll neck) Size 18 tapestry needle

Gauge:
With larger size needles in stockinette stitch (knit one row, purl one row):
17 sts = 4"

Instructions

Back
With smaller size straight needles, cast on 28 sts.

Ribbing:
Row 1: * K1, P1; rep from * across.

Rows 2 through 5: Rep Row 1.

Row 6: K1, (P1, K1) 4 times; M1 (see Special Abbreviations); * (P1, K1) 5 times, M1; (P1, K1) 4 times; P1—30 sts.

Change to larger size needles.

Body:
Row 1 (right side): Knit.

Row 2: Purl.

Rep Rows 1 and 2 until piece measures about 3" from cast-on edge, ending by working a wrong side row.

Armhole Shaping:
Row 1 (right side): Bind off 1 st, knit across.

Row 2: Bind off 1 st, purl across—28 sts.

Row 3: Purl.

Row 4: Knit.

Row 5: Knit.

Row 6: Purl.

Row 7: K1; * P2, K2; rep from * to last 3 sts; P2, K1.

Row 8: Purl.

Row 9: K3; * P2, K2; rep from * to last 5 sts; P2, K3.

Row 10: Purl.

Rows 11 through 18: Rep Rows 7 through 10 twice more.

Rows 19 and 20: Rep Rows 7 and 8.

Row 21: Purl.

Row 22: Knit.

Bind off.

Front

Work same as Back to Armhole Shaping.

Armhole Shaping:

Row 1 (right side): Bind off one st, knit across.

Row 2: Bind off one st, purl across—28 sts.

Row 3: Purl.

Row 4: Knit.

Row 5: Knit.

Row 6: Purl.

Row 7: K1; * P2, K2; rep from * to last 3 sts; P2, K1.

Row 8: Purl.

Row 9: K3; * P2, K2; rep from * to last 5 sts; P2, K3.

Row 10: Purl.

Neck Shaping:

Row 1 (right side): For left shoulder, K1, P2, K2, P2, K3; join second skein of yarn; for neck, bind off 8 sts; for right shoulder, K3, P2, K2, P2, K1—10 sts on each shoulder.

Note: *Work both shoulders at same time with separate skeins of yarn.*

Rows 2, 4, 6 and 8: Purl.

Row 3: For left shoulder, K3, P2, K2, K2 tog; K1; for right shoulder, K1, SSK (see Special Abbreviations); K2, P2, K3—9 sts on each shoulder.

Row 5: For left shoulder, K1, P2, K3, K2 tog; K1; for right shoulder, K1, SSK; K3, P2, K1—8 sts on each shoulder.

Row 7: For left shoulder, K3, P2, K2 tog; K1; for right shoulder, K1, SSK; P2, K3—7 sts on each shoulder.

Row 9: For left shoulder, K1, P2, K4; for right shoulder, K4, P2, K1.

Row 10: Purl.

Row 11: Purl.

Row 12: Knit.

Bind off.

Sew shoulder seams.

Sleeve

With smaller size straight needles, pick up 26 sts evenly spaced along armhole edge beginning and ending above bound off sts of armhole shaping and having same number of sts on front and back.

Change to larger size needles.

Row 1 (wrong side): Knit.

Row 2 (right side): Purl.

Rows 3, 5, 7, 9: Purl.

Row 4: K1; SSK; K1; * P2, K2; rep from * to last 6 sts; P2, K1, K2 tog; K1—24 sts.

Row 6: K1; * P2, K2; rep from * to last 3 sts; P2, K1.

Row 8: K3; * P2, K2; rep from * to last 5 sts; P2, K3.

Row 10: K1, SSK; knit to last 3 sts; K2 tog; K1—22 sts.

Row 11: Knit.

Row 12: Purl.

Row 13: Purl.

Row 14: Knit.

Row 15: Purl.

Row 16: K1, SSK; knit to last 3 sts; K2 tog; K1—21 sts.

Row 17: Purl.

Rows 19 through 36: Rep Rows 13 through 18 three times more. At end of Row 36—18 sts.

Rep Rows 13 and 14 until sleeve measures about 3¾", ending by working a wrong side row.

Row 37: K5, K2 tog; K4, K2 tog; K5—16 sts.

Change to smaller size needles.

Ribbing:

Row 1 (right side): * K1, P1; rep from * across.

Rows 2 through 5:

Rep Row 1.

Bind off loosely in ribbing.

Rep for other sleeve.

Sew side and sleeve seams.

Neck Edging:

Hold piece with right side facing you and neck edge at top; with double-pointed needles pick up 40 sts evenly spaced around neck edge.

Rnd 1: * K1, P1; rep from * across.

Rnds 2 through 7: Rep Rnd 1.

Bind off loosely in ribbing.

Cool Blue Gansey (for child)

▮▮▮▮▯ INTERMEDIATE

Sizes:

2 4 6 8 10 12

Finished Chest Size:

27" 28½" 30" 32" 34" 37"

Note: Instructions are written for Size 2; changes for other sizes are in parentheses.

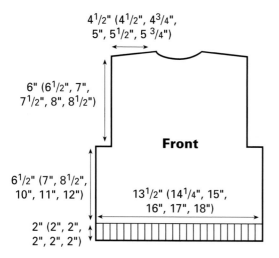

4½" (4½", 4¾", 5", 5½", 5¾")

6" (6½", 7", 7½", 8", 8½")

Front

6½" (7", 8½", 10", 11", 12")

13½" (14¼", 15", 16", 17", 18")

2" (2", 2", 2", 2", 2")

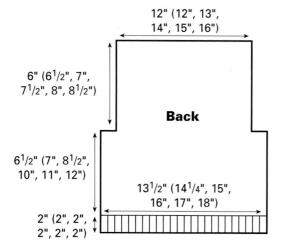

12" (12", 13", 14", 15", 16")

6" (6½", 7", 7½", 8", 8½")

Back

6½" (7", 8½", 10", 11", 12")

13½" (14¼", 15", 16", 17", 18")

2" (2", 2", 2", 2", 2")

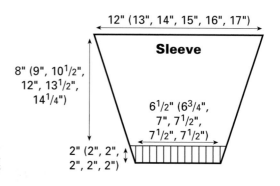

12" (13", 14", 15", 16", 17")

Sleeve

8" (9", 10½", 12", 13½", 14¼")

6½" (6¾", 7", 7½", 7½", 7½")

2" (2", 2", 2", 2", 2")

These measurements for child's sweater sizes are approximate.

Materials:
Light (worsted weight) yarn, 10 (15, 15, 20, 20, 25) oz [472 (708, 708, 944, 944, 1180) yds, 284 (426, 426, 568, 568, 710) gms] blue
Note: Our photographed sweater was made with Lion Brand Cotton Ease, Ice Blue #106.
Size 8 (5mm) knitting needles, or size required for gauge
Size 5 (3.75mm) straight knitting needle
Size 5 (3.75mm) circular needle (for neck)
Size 18 tapestry needle

Gauge:
With larger size needles in stockinette stitch (knit one row, purl one row):
4 sts = 1"

Make 1 (M1):
Insert left needle from front to back under horizontal strand between the last stitch worked and the next stitch on the left needle; knit this strand through the back loop—M1 made.

Slip, Slip, Knit (SSK):
Slip next 2 sts one at a time from the left needle to the right needle, insert the left needle into the fronts of these two stitches and knit them together—SSK made.

Instructions

Back
With smaller size straight needles, cast on 52 (56, 58, 62, 66, 68) sts.

Ribbing:
Row 1: * K1, P1; rep from * across.

Rows 2 through 11: Rep Row 1.

Next Row: Continuing in pattern as established, work 6 (6, 7, 6, 6, 5) sts, M1 (see Special Abbreviations); * work 8 (9, 9, 10, 11, 9) sts, M1; rep from * 4 (4, 4, 4, 4, 6) times more; work 6 (5, 6, 6, 5, 4)—58 (62, 64, 68, 72, 76) sts.

Change to larger size needles.

Body:
Row 1 (right side): Knit.

Row 2: Purl.

Rep Rows 1 and 2 until piece measures about 8½" (9", 10½", 12", 13", 14") from cast-on edge, ending by working a wrong side row.

Armhole Shaping:
Row 1 (right side): Bind off 3 (5, 4, 4, 4, 4) sts; knit across.

Row 2: Bind off 3 (5, 4, 4, 4, 4) sts; purl across—52 (52, 56, 60, 64, 68) sts.

Row 3: Purl.

Row 4: Knit.

Row 5: Knit.

Row 6: Purl.

Row 7: K1; * P2, K2; rep from * to last 3 sts; P2, K1.

Row 8: Purl.

Row 9: K3; * P2, K2; rep from * to last 5 sts; P2, K3.

Row 10: Purl.

Rows 11 through 18 (18, 22, 22, 22, 26): Rep Rows 7 through 10 two (2, 3, 3, 3, 4) times more.

For Sizes 2, 6, 8 and 12 Only:
Rows 19 (23, 23, 27) through 34 (42, 42, 50): Rep Rows 3 through 18 (22, 22, 26) once.

Next Row: Purl.

Next Row: Knit.

Bind off.

Continue with Front below.

For Sizes 4 and 10 Only:
Rows 19 (23) and 20 (24): Rep Rows 7 and 8.

Rows 21 (25) through 38 (46): Rep Rows 3 through 20 (24) once.

Next Row: Purl.

Next Row: Knit.

Bind off.

Continue with Front.

Front
Work same as Back to Armhole Shaping.

Armhole Shaping:
Row 1 (right side): Bind off 3 (5, 4, 4, 4, 4) sts; knit across.

Row 2: Bind off 3 (5, 4, 4, 4, 4) sts; purl across—52 (52, 56, 60, 64, 68) sts.

Row 3: Purl.

Row 4: Knit.

Row 5: Knit.

Row 6: Purl.

Row 7: K1; * P2, K2; rep from * to last 3 sts; P2, K1.

Row 8: Purl.

Row 9: K3; * P2, K2; rep from * to last 5 sts; P2, K3.

Row 10: Purl.

Rows 11 through 18 (18, 22, 22, 22, 26): Rep Rows 7 through 10 two (2, 3, 3, 3, 4) times more.

For Sizes 2, 6, 8, and 12 Only:

Row 19 (23, 23, 27): Purl.

Row 20 (24, 24, 28): Knit.

Continue with Neck Shaping below.

For Sizes 4 and 10 Only:

Rows 19 (23) and 20 (24): Rep Rows 7 and 8.

Rows 21 (25): Purl.

Row 22 (26): Knit.

Continue with Neck Shaping.

Neck Shaping:

Row 1 (right side): For left shoulder, K20 (20, 21, 23, 25, 26) sts; join second skein of yarn; bind off 12 (12, 14, 14, 14, 16) sts for neck; knit rem sts—20 (20, 21, 23, 25, 26) sts on each shoulder.

Note: Work both shoulders at same time with separate skeins of yarn.

Row 2: Purl across both shoulders.

Continuing in pattern as established.

Row 3: For left shoulder, work in pattern to last 4 sts; K2 tog; K2; for right shoulder, K2, SSK (see Special Abbreviations); work in pattern across—19 (19, 20, 22, 24, 25) sts on each shoulder.

Row 4: Purl across both shoulders.

Rows 5 through 14: Rep Rows 3 and 4 five time more. At end of Row 13—14 (14, 15, 17, 19, 20) sts.

If necessary, work even (without dec) in pattern until front has 2 rows less than back shoulder, ending by working a wrong side row.

Next Row: Purl across both shoulders.

Next Row: Knit across both shoulders.

Bind off.

Sew shoulder seams.

Sleeve

With smaller size straight needles, pick up 52 (56, 60, 64, 68, 72) sts evenly spaced along armhole edge beginning and ending above bound off sts of armhole shaping and having same number of sts on front and back.

Change to larger size needles.

Row 1 (wrong side): Knit.

Row 2 (right side): Purl.

Rows 3, 5, 7, 9, 11, 13, 15 and 17: Purl.

Row 4: K1; * P2, K2; rep from * to last 3 sts; P2, K1.

Row 6: K3; * P2, K2; rep from * to last 5 sts; P2, K3.

Row 8: K2, SSK; K1; * P2, K2; rep from * to last 5 sts; K1, K2 tog; K2—50 (54, 58, 62, 66, 70) sts.

Row 10: * K2, P2; rep from * to last 2 sts; K2.

Row 12: K2, SSK; * P2, K2; rep from * to last 6 sts; P2, K2 tog; K2—48 (52, 56, 60, 64, 68) sts.

Row 14: K1; * P2, K2; rep from * to last 3 sts; P2, K1.

Row 16: K2, SSK, P1; * P2, K2; rep from * to last 7 sts; K1, P1, K2 tog; K2—46 (50, 54, 58, 62, 66) sts.

Row 18: K4; * P2, K2; rep from * to last 6 sts; P2, K4.

Row 19: Purl.

For Sizes 2 and 4 Only:

Row 20 (right side): P2, P2 tog; purl to last 4 sts; P2 tog tbl; P2—44 (48) sts.

Row 21: Knit.

Continue with For All Sizes below.

For Sizes 6 and 8 Only:

Row 20 (right side): K2, SSK; K2; * P2, K2; rep from * to last 4 sts; K2 tog; K2—52 (56) sts.

Rows 21: Purl.

Row 22: K3; * P2, K2; rep from * to last 5 sts; P2, K3.

Row 23: Purl.

Row 24: P2, P2 tog; purl to last 4 sts; P2 tog tbl; P2—50 (54) sts.

Row 25: Knit.

Continue with For All Sizes below.